Master
of
Circumstance

ISBN 978-1-954095-20-5 (Paperback)
Master of Circumstance
Copyright © 2021 James Morgan

Yorkshire Publishing
1425 E 41st Pl
Tulsa, OK 74105
www.YorkshirePublishing.com
918.394.2665

Printed in the USA

Master
of
Circumstance

Shattering the 7 Illusions

That Stop You from Living Life Intentionally

James Morgan

TULSA

I'd like to dedicate this book to the woman who came into my life and changed me forever, my wife Sandra. She challenged me the day we married by asking me what the future holds for us. It was then I knew I wanted a forever with her. Summer of our first year of marriage she came home from work with a design for the cover of the book that I had never even thought about writing. This was 2002. She said "after all you've been through, I think you'll have a great story to tell, because you never let things get you down". All the circumstances that have come against you, you've never been a victim to them, more of a master if you ask me. A master of circumstance. I'd also like to acknowledge the role my daughter Amanda and son William have had on the writing of this book. Amanda was the center of my world and then it all fell apart when the pressures of living in two separate homes with an antagonistic relationship between the parents existed. Through all my best efforts, I destroyed our relationship and failed her as a father. I learned a lot of what not to do with children and how important it is to check in to ensure the message being sent is the message being received. With William, he is the best part of me. He is the culmination of all my mistakes with Amanda and the loving nature of his mother. He is boy of extraordinary character beyond his years. He has taught me how to be more forgiving of others and myself. He challenges me in every way by the questions he asks and how he sees the world. This life that we live now, together, is the best I could have ever imagined. Sandra, Amanda, and William have all been a part of the growth I've experienced. I'm extremely grateful for their forgiveness and unconditional love that they've shown me.

Love Daddio

CONTENTS

FOREWORD

What keeps most people from living their best life and achieving everything they dream of for themselves? It's not money. It's not education. It's not who their parents are (or are not). It's not where or when they are born. It comes down to one thing. How they think. How they think about themselves and others.

As a coach and speaker over the past 15 years, I've seen too many people get stuck because they thought they were powerless. On the contrary, we all have the power to change. We all have the power to live life with satisfaction, success and significance.

James Morgan discovered this for himself and when he did, his life was changed forever. Years later he is still applying what he learned and helping others discover it for themselves. That is why James wrote this book. He didn't just come up with these theories. He unearthed them within his own life experiences and now he shares those discoveries with you.

As a very good friend and mentor of mine says, "Beliefs drive behavior". You are holding in your hands a very important tool in helping you discover what beliefs are driving your behavior. Understanding that alone is enough to shift your thinking. It is enough to shift how to view the behavior of others and give them grace for not being aware of how their behavior is impacting everyone around them.

The argument of nature vs. nurture has been going on for eons and has yet to be truly resolved. Here is what I do know. We are complex beings with layers of beliefs distorting our view of ourselves and the world around us. Understanding ourselves is the first step in taking responsibility for ourselves and the results we get in our life to live our best life. James helps you peel back the layers of the onion until you get to the core of your beliefs, and your power to change. The power to become a master of your circumstance.

We can't control other people. We can't control the economy. We can't control interest rates. The ONLY thing we can completely control is our own thinking. We can always choose how we respond. We can always choose our behavior. Behavior that is self-serving rather than self-defeating.

Socrates once said, "an unexamined life is not worth living". People who understand what drives their behavior are the ones who take that inward journey and examine themselves and their life. They have to intentionally make that choice every day if they are ever to live their best life.

My guess is if you are reading this book, you want to do that too. In a time when so many feel like a victim being buffeted about by the sudden and often challenging changes going on around them, you don't have to be one of them.

James will show you how as he shares both his victories and his setbacks and what he has learned from each. I encourage you to get ready to dig deep and then apply what you discover. I promise you it will be well worth the effort.

Chris Robinson
Executive Vice President
Maxwell Entrepreneurial Solutions

CHAPTER ONE

It Doesn't Have to Be This Way

"Life can only be understood backwards;
but it must be lived forwards."
-Søren Kierkegaard

Master (*noun*)
1.1 A person who has complete control of something.
"He was master of the situation"

I was sitting in the passenger seat of a pickup truck going over a country road in Illinois when my buddy asked me if I'd go to church with him. As a licensed therapist, I can't advocate for any one particular religion over another, but I can tell you how I responded on that day 20 years ago. "Well, clearly what I've been doing doesn't work, so I guess I'm open to trying something different."

You don't have to go to church to change your life. But you do need to do something different than you've ever done before if you want to see different results. When I agreed to go with my buddy to his church on Sunday, while riding shotgun on the bumpy backroads of Illinois, I was far from being a master of my circumstance. To put it plainly, I was lost.

Twenty-nine years old, an inch from filing for bankruptcy, divorced not once, not twice, but three times, and I'd been fired from more jobs than the number of years I'd been alive. It wouldn't be a stretch to say that I was a wreck of a human being. I needed a change and, for me, showing up at church was the much-needed answer to my proverbial prayers.

As you read this book, you may have a few doubts about the current circumstances of your life right now. But the question you have to ask yourself is this: *Is what you are doing working to get you what you want out of life?* My guess is that it's not. I have some good news for you, though: *it doesn't have to be this way.*

If I've learned one thing as a therapist, it is that behind every person who walks into my counseling practice there is a slight feeling of existential despair. (Yep, I know what you're thinking—*this guy turned out to be a therapist?!* Actually, it turns out that being a horrible person and overcoming your own CRAP can make you pretty good at helping other people to see theirs. It also pays a lot better than working at Gitcho's Gas Station.)

In some clients, existential despair is so subtle that it is almost imperceptible. In others, it's written right on their sleeve for everyone in their life to see, except for them. No matter who we are or what we do, there's an uncertainty hiding within us all about what our purpose is and how we can live the lives we were meant to lead.

Now, the type of despair I'm talking about most likely doesn't involve a lot of sulking and crying; it's more along the lines of an unconscious habit. You could even say that it is something we've just accepted as the way things are. For a long time in my life, I simply accepted my bad attitude, my ability to get fired from jobs, blowing up relationships, and TORCHING bridges as just who I was. *That's just the way it is* might as well have been written down in my will as what should go on my tombstone. However, the more I worked through those unconscious habits and thoughts, the more I realized that I wasn't excited about my life, and my boredom caused me to search out trouble.

"At dawn, when you have trouble getting out of bed, tell yourself: "I have to go to work—as a human being. What do I have to complain of, if I'm going to do what I was born for—the things I was brought into the world to do? Or is this what I was created for? To huddle under the blankets and stay warm?" So, you were born to feel "nice"? Instead of doing things and experiencing them?

People who love what they do wear themselves down
doing it; they even forget to wash or eat."
Marcus Aurelius, Meditations

The above quote from Marcus Aurelius sums up the tension between what we want our lives to look like and the fear of change and facing what we don't know. Mystery and the unknown permeate everything we do in life without our even being able to consciously recognize it. If we can't pinpoint it for what it is, it continues to go undiagnosed and this uncertainty eventually seeps into our relationships, our careers, and our personal aspirations. We quickly learn to cover this up. And, the better we get at covering it up, the more it masks our true potential from shining through.

Take it from me. I was virtually unemployable, undatable, and unapologetic about being a jerk about all of it. Today, I run a business that supports several families, including my own. To get to where I am today, I had to dig deep, deeper than I ever had before, and start asking the really hard questions.

"Does It Really Have to Be This Way?"

I was sick of resigning myself to a life that looked like Bill Murray in the movie *Groundhog Day*. Every day was just an endless loop of me doing the same stupid stuff to sabotage my life while thinking that something outside of me was going to change me. So many people today resist change. They wake up every single morning and do the same things without even thinking about it, just on autopilot. The title of this book is about *mastery*. On the surface, it may seem like it's just another self-help book about finding your *#bestself*. In reality, it's about acceptance of your worst self, so that you can move past it.

There's a hard truth we all must learn at some point in our lives: You can't control your circumstances but you can control yourself. To do this, you have to remove the resistance, the *"it is what it is"* mentality. Because, at its core, that is just an excuse. It's a false sense of acceptance that is probably holding you back from getting where you want to go. You have to let go of your attachment to the outcome before you can truly own your actions.

Disclaimer: There is no fancy 90-day money-back guarantee stamped on the back cover of this book because the truth is you can do everything perfectly and still jack it all up. For instance, you can drink gallons of freshly squeezed carrot juice for breakfast, run five miles a day, never smoke, never touch a drop of alcohol, be in bed by 9:30 pm, live a stress-free life and still die of cancer after a horribly painful battle. I'm not being flippant, I'm being realistic.

There's a greater philosophical truth at work that doesn't take into account how many pull-ups you can do, or what your cholesterol is: *Meaning can be derived only from your own choices and how you feel about them.* I'm not saying to neglect your health and be Keith Richards—although Keith Richards seems pretty happy—I'm saying that all you can control is the way you act in the world. You don't get to choose how it impacts the world around you.

So, what does that mean? It means that you can't control what happens to you, the circumstances that you're thrown into, no matter what you do. However, even though cause and effect isn't always a perfect 100% match of expectation with reality, they do add up most of the time. For example, how many smokers have you heard of who died of lung cancer? Probably quite a few. It may not mean that you will get cancer, but it increases the likelihood. Similarly, there are probably a lot of *illusions* that you are living with that keep you blind to what is really going on in your heart, in your head, and in your interactions with the outside world. In this book, the goal will be to elucidate how you are diminishing your chances of mastery and how you can maximize your outcome so that you get the best shot at living masterfully.

The Illusion of Maya

Some Vedic teachings say that the world is an illusion called *Maya*. This suggests that the world isn't actually what we can physically see, that there is more behind it than meets the eye. The reason I wrote this book is that I believe most of us are blind to the unconscious blocks that hijack our truth. We believe that someone else is to blame for our failures. Or we falsely expect that something outside of ourselves will make us happy, even though it's actually just a societal pressure. Maybe we feel that we can never be as good as we could have been because guilt is eating away at us. Or perhaps we just can't stomach the fact that someone else could be right and we could be wrong. These illusions are easy to believe. They are mostly formed in childhood and a lot of them are learned behaviors.

If I asked you to tie your shoes, you could probably do that pretty quickly. But if I asked you to tie your shoes a different way, it may take you a while. That's the hard work of this book. Mastery means overcoming the easy, unconscious ways of acting that are creating havoc in your life and holding you back from actually living intentionally.

Our Memory Isn't Reliable

I want you to think about a few of the things that are driving you nuts about your current circumstances for a moment. Go ahead, picture them in your mind. Have you ever thought about how your actions and the way you recall your actions probably aren't *100%* the same thing?

The fact is, memory is unreliable. From client stories during therapy to eye-witness police reports—we know that memory isn't always accurate. In fact, it is always colored to match your bias. So, if you are a person, assuming you aren't a chimpanzee or a really smart talking parrot, it's probably pretty safe to say that not everything you remember about your life is correct. As a result, your current biases could probably be called into question.

In *The Mind Explained* docu-series, researchers explain how memories are made and show that memory is completely unreliable because of the very process by which memories work inside the brain. When the researchers in the film conducted an *fMRI* on the brain, they found two areas of the brain that light up when memories are being made. *Can you guess what else gets created in those two areas of the brain?* Your imagination.

That's right. Right next to your memory vault is a little Mickey Mouse wearing a Fantasia hat and conjuring up all sorts of fictitious thoughts about what you are trying to process as facts about how your life has happened so far. This accounts for why, as humans, we have a very hard time between *did that really happen* or *did I just make that up?* This not only makes it tough on you, but it also makes it tough on your therapist, too!

This is an important aspect of this book because so many of us are convinced that *I have this right, I remember it* correctly. I'm not saying that *all* of our memories are wrong or that we shouldn't trust our firsthand accounts of our lives. Quite the contrary. What I'm actually suggesting is that maybe there is another way to think about it.

We don't think about our experiences in terms of *"I do this thing I do because of this other thing that happened to me that I can't even remember."* Instead, we accept that our memory is the way it happened and then we go into interpretation mode. We don't stop and ask questions such as: *What does this mean? What does that say about me? What did I do wrong? What should I do differently?* It becomes concrete; it's your reality. And now it gets stored in the subconscious.

Remember, our memories and our past create maps for the future. One of the most important aspects that I will cover later on in this book is the topic of expectations. Just because you know how something has ended before, it doesn't mean that it has to end that way again this time. However, our expectations lead us to write off our future before we even wake up in the morning! As in the Marcus Aurelius quote, we don't even want to get out of bed because our bodies are programmed as to how they think our future will look. To change your life, you have to change your expectations and, to do that, you have to change your perception of your circumstances. For almost every circumstance in your life, you could ask yourself the following questions:

Is that really what Happened?
Is that true?
*What was **my role** in this?*

Why have I settled for this?
Where did I learn this?
Why am I saying this is as good as it gets?
Is it possible that everything I've seen in my life is viewed through a broken lens that created my thoughts, my experiences, and my past?

Chances are, this mindset has permeated every aspect of your life. Don't worry if a lot of the questions above seem scary, that's just the fear of change rearing its ugly head. This book is about you taking control and becoming responsible for your life. Responsibility always comes at the price of action.

The Seven Victim Mindsets

I can sniff out BS a mile away—I mean it's like a sixth sense. My mother was a single mom and an alcoholic. I never even knew my dad's name until the day I enlisted in the Navy. For years, my mom would make up stories about who he was or flat out ignore the question entirely, telling me that I didn't need to know. Statistically speaking, the fact that I escaped minimum-wage work and got out of the negative cycle of dysfunction was a miracle. As a result, I know when somebody is lying. You see, my mother was a victim and she was always the one being wronged or hurt in almost every circumstance. So naturally, I went out into the world and I made every mistake possible. Every time something went wrong, I played the victim card. Until one day, I realized that I wasn't getting any younger and life wasn't getting any easier. It wasn't until I started to realize the foundations for the seven victim mindsets I explain in this book that

I was able to change. Once I started seeing them show up in my own life, I quickly began to change and get my act together. Let's dig in and diagnose where we're at so we can figure out how to get out of this.

Some books only have one good reason to read them. This one will have seven. One of the things that I have to make clear up front is that no one would ever be a victim if they didn't think it was serving them. Reread that sentence. It might sound a little strange at first but no one would ever feel victimized if they didn't think that it was doing them some good on some level. In fact, being a victim is like having an airbag: It protects you from the blow of crashing into your own truth. It's your brain's natural defense system to keep you safe from the danger of the unknown.

Essentially, this book is just a useful tool to help you deal with the unknown. Because every time one of us goes into a victim mindset, it is to protect ourselves from one thing—the unknown. Disclaimer: I'm not talking about the physical act of being a victim. If you are mugged, assaulted, beat up—you actually are a victim, and please seek out the proper authorities immediately. I'm talking about what shows up afterward and gets played in your head. Here's an analogy for how being a victim shows up in your daily life.

Imagine that you were in a serious car accident and the airbag went off. At first, it was painful—the pressure comes out at you at a whopping 200 miles per hour—*bam!* Right to the face. It's a shock for sure, but the reward is that you are still alive. You get out of your car and you realize that you are lucky to walk away unharmed. But imagine that, after you filed the police report and the mechanics started loading your car onto the tow truck, you stopped dead in your tracks. Terror set in. Your brain fired rapidly, looking for answers to this question: *What if this happens to me again? What will I do?*

A moment of panic washes over you. You do the first thing that comes to your mind. *Sprint!*

As you run up to the tow truck, you start banging on the back for them to let you get just one last thing out of your car. Of course, they oblige—it's your car, after all—and as you walk away, the onlookers who have gathered around look confused.

"Mommy why is that person carrying around an airbag on their head?" a small child asks.

"I don't know son, maybe they hit their head too hard."

It might sound silly, but victimhood is a lot like the above example. We carry around something that worked for us in one situation that caused us extreme pain and use it as a crutch to protect us in every incidence that we *think* is similar. Even when the situation isn't going to hurt us, we may try to make ourselves believe that it is, just so we can be absolutely sure.

Like a one-hit wonder, we keep playing the same song, five, ten, fifteen, twenty, fifty years later expecting it to still work, but as Bob Dylan put it, *"The times they are a-changin'"* except we haven't changed.

"Hey, look there's Bob."

"What's he carrying around that airbag for?"

"Oh, that's just his thing. That's just the way he is."

What Bob doesn't realize is that he is not only walking around with an airbag on his head, he is also wearing glasses that are colored to only see threats. However, being a victim isn't all bad. In fact, it can be the road sign that leads you toward knowing where you want to go in life and which road to choose.

The purpose of this book is to help you recognize where you choose victimhood, so that you can try something else. Just like that moment in the truck with my friend when I realized that *what I was currently doing wasn't working and maybe it was time to try something else*, you can move past your former obstacles faster than you ever dreamed possible. That being said, that's just one possible outcome. For every victim mentality, there are actually two paths.

On the first path, you wake up and realize that you are risking some pretty great stuff by staying in the victim mentality. When you become aware of this risk, you can choose to change your behavior and receive your Masterful divine right—just like the kings in ancient times, you too have a right to feel free. On the other path, you can also choose to ignore the risks completely and get the unconscious reward that tricks you into playing the victim.

Victim Mindset 1 — Blame (Power) {Powerlessness}

Mastering your circumstances isn't easy. It starts with accepting some basic truths about yourself that can feel pretty *crappy* at first. That's normal. In fact, it's so normal that you've probably got used to *accepting* some insane lies about yourself as your own truth, because you were stuck in mediocrity. Don't worry, it happens to all of us. One of these truths is that you blame: people, governments, God, the sky, the weather—anything that lets you off the hook and makes you feel more in control. A lot of people in the world today are running around blaming a lot of other people for their actions. Just like Morpheus in *The Matrix,* you have two options. Behind one hand is the blue easy-to-swallow pill, which you can choose to take.

My dad never loved me. He never gave me the attention I deserve. My mom never bought me anything. I'd be better looking if I had better clothes growing up. My partner is the reason I lose my temper. If she wouldn't do that, I wouldn't have to get so mad.

These are excuses that don't really hold up. However, every single day, somebody somewhere is using a similar excuse as their reason not to become the master over the circumstances they've been dealt. They are still the red-faced little boy or girl who points a finger, and throws a temper tantrum, saying, *"They started it."* It might work at five years old, but at forty-five it isn't cute.

If you choose to take the blue pill (to accept your excuses) you fall victim to the unconscious reward. When we don't get over our blame and step into our power, we become powerless.

You see, blame gets rid of our responsibility and, without responsibility, we don't have the power to take action. When you can't act, you can't get what you want, so you continue to do what comes easiest, which is blame other people. That way, you never have to be the one in charge and you can never get in trouble for not having the things you want because you couldn't get them anyway. Now, that's a doozy of a story!

When you are known as a blamer, your friends and family won't want to be around you, because they will be afraid that you'll blame them for what's going wrong in your life. They'll be worried that they'll be next on your hit list. Blame comes disguised as power but, in reality, it strips you of all credibility because you can't accept the consequences of your own actions.

Victim Mindset 2 — Expectation (Choice) {Helplessness}

I think it was the Buddha who said, *"Peace begins when expectations end."* When we have expectations about ourselves that we hold as our truth, it limits and distorts our reality. How? Our reality is distorted when we live in illusion instead of accepting how things actually are. Now, just as in blame, there are again two paths to travel.

On the first path, we realize that we can't control the outcomes of our actions; we can only make the conscious choice of how to act. Additionally, when we drop our expectations, we let go of a whole slew of other baggage that is holding us back in life. But, if we can't loosen our grip on our expectations, we become helpless, which is the second path. In our own fixed belief about what reality should be, we can't accept our current situation and we feel trapped by the beliefs that we thought were really helping us.

Expectations are tricky because they can be entangled with our dreams and visions for the future. However, sometimes what we think are our dreams are actually self-imposed limitations. This isn't something you can just arrive at overnight. It will take a lot of introspection and self-awareness to get there, but it could be something that is seriously holding you back.

Questions to ask yourself are: Why do I never feel good enough? Why do I never feel like I am doing it right? Why do I never feel like I am doing it as well as everyone else?

Then ask yourself: Whose expectations are you following? Are they your parent's expectations? Are they your expectations or your spouse's expectations? Or society's expectations? *How do our unconscious expectations play out and hold us back?*

Pretend that you were an ambitious seven-year-old girl who wanted to be a singer. You were good at dancing, and your mom and Dad loved watching you sing for them. *Isn't she cute!?* However, fast-forward ten years to when you worked toward that dream. Your friends were all having fun and dating in high school and you were working the bar circuit with a legal chaperone on the weekends before you were even old enough to drink. Dance rehearsals kept you up until 9 pm every night and, by the time you commuted back home, you were too exhausted to do your homework. As a result, your grades fell below your mother's expectation that you would go to a prestigious college, so you began thinking about dropping out of high school. Fast-forward another ten years and you are working at nightclubs, bars, and odd jobs to make ends meet while trying to save enough money for studio time.

When you wanted to be the next pop star Britney Spears as a seven-year-old girl, you probably weren't thinking about everything that came with it. As a twenty-seven-year-old, however, you may no longer want to be the next Britney Spears. In reality, all of the stress, the grueling dance rehearsals, the constant rejection, and the creative blocks just don't add up the way you thought they would. Now, when you decide to go back to school to pursue another passion in your late twenties, you feel like a failure.

The reality is that you had an expectation at seven years old that being a pop star would be the best course for your life. But did you really understand what Britney Spears or Madonna were going through? At seven years old, you didn't even know what a martini was, let alone what real stress was. You didn't know anything about the realities that come with stardom or what it would take to get there. You only had an expectation about what you thought it meant.

So, no, your expectation did not meet reality. Now, stay with me for a minute. It goes even deeper.

At twenty-seven, your expectation that you will be a pop star still stems from a belief that you had at seven. And, if you decide to do something that would be a better move for you, more aligned with what you actually want for your life, you may feel resentment toward yourself.

Ah, the question is why? Because your self-expectation at seven years old is limiting your reality and making you live in an illusion. That's pretty crazy, huh?

Think about this concept: A lot of us feel helpless because we don't have a good relationship with our parents. But there is no law that says you have to have a perfect relationship with your parents.

In fact, having a good relationship with your parents is just a societal expectation. If you have a toxic relationship with your parents, it may be better for you not to interact. Society's expectation is that you should fight like hell to make your relationship work. But what I want you to know is that it's okay if it doesn't and dropping that expectation can lead you onto the yellow brick road to following your own truth.

Victim Mindset 3 — Guilt (Peace) {Chaos}

Ah, if there is one thing that can debilitate a person, it is guilt. Guilt will rob you of peace faster than any of the other seven victim mindsets. Guilt is the only one that will make you feel ashamed. And, when you feel shame, it is impossible to have peace because you can't be at peace with yourself. This is an important distinction because it manifests itself as something that we hold against ourselves. Guilt wraps us up in regret.

What are you missing out on because of the guilt that you have from the way that you've lived your life so far? When you are living in guilt and living in regret because of that guilt, there is no way that you can possibly sense at a deeper level all of the good stuff that is going on around you. Now, guilt might form from unconscious expectations that we have, or from blaming other people, or from any of the other victim mindsets, but many of us cling to guilt as a way not to be able to have peace.

Now, why would we do this?

Feeling guilty allows us to hold onto the expectation. Then we feel that, since we are guilty, we don't deserve the things we really want, so we make ourselves feel better about not having them. Shame and embarrassment combine to add to the weight of guilt. The weightiness of guilt is suffocating your life. So, let me ask you this: *Who haven't you been because of your guilt? Who haven't you been for your children? For your spouse? For yourself? Were you the most productive you could have been while hanging onto the crushing weight of guilt? Could you have made more of the opportunities you've had during the years of feeling guilty?* If you want to find out where you feel guilty ask yourself: *Where do you feel like you aren't enough?* Then you'll find your answer.

It is likely that guilt causes you to be blocked in your life in several key areas. It can show up in your relationships, your career, or your overall mood. When this happens, it can be very difficult to track down, because you have probably grown accustomed to just feeling like this. It feels very *you* and *it is just the way it is.*

Guilt is secretive and it hides you from yourself. But it doesn't hide the bad stuff, that's the illusion. The truth is that it hides the goodness of yourself from you because it masks all the positive aspects of who you really are. Then it conceals the truth of who you are, which is your inner peace. To keep yourself from that truth, you will create chaos in your life, because you don't want to recognize it.

Victim Mindset 4 — Being Overwhelmed (Control) {Out of control}

Corporate burnout is a popular topic in today's world. With employees being glued to their phones and reachable twenty-four hours a day, it is impossible to separate work and personal life sometimes, which is probably what comes to mind when you think about being overwhelmed. The topic goes far beyond just work, though. In fact, this victim mindset can sneak into almost any aspect of your life and sabotage it.

How?

Often, being overwhelmed can become an excuse for not having control of our lives or (more likely) not wanting to take control of our lives. It can be a way for us to shirk our responsibilities and it is very much self-inflicted.

The basic psychology behind being overwhelmed works like this: "I am not enough. And when I'm not enough, I get rejected. So I either avoid relationships completely to avoid that rejection, or I *do, do, do,* to look good and avoid rejection."

That's the drive. It creates pressure to do, which then causes us to make mistakes. That's when we start to sabotage ourselves because we continue to act like it's all too much, make mistakes, and get rejected. Then, when we inevitably fail, we can easily write it off as having been overwhelmed instead of taking responsibility for our actions and creating something better for our lives.

The secret to being overwhelmed is that most people don't know it's a learned behavior. It's also a very stressful behavior. *Ahh! There's so much going on, I can't do anymore!* This is a learned response—you can most likely thank your parents. Whoever you can picture saying the above phrase in an upset exaggerated sigh—they're to *"blame."* *Just kidding!* You can either focus on the storm you are in and watch the clouds swarm over your head or you can focus on solutions and get to safety. A lot of people get irritable when they are overwhelmed; they get short-sighted and act sporadically. They take actions that aren't necessarily in line with what they would do if they weren't under that inferred pressure of being overwhelmed.

Victim Mindset 5 — Confusion (Confidence) {Insecure}

Confusion is one of the most easily cured of the seven victim mindsets, but it is also the least recognizable. A lot of my clients defend their confusion because they don't see how it is serving them unconsciously. They don't progress or move things forward, because they claim to be confused.

When you say *I don't know*, it can't get you into trouble because *who could possibly blame you for not knowing something?* The unintended consequence is that you get attention. You get to play the victim. You get to avoid responsibility. And you get others to help you or do the work for you.

Confusion allows us to ignore fear of something. It could be fear of consequences. Fear of the next step. Fear of risk. Fear of the unknown and uncertainty. It allows us to neglect things that we really don't want to be responsible for in the first place. Then we get to ask for other people's sympathy or their compassion.

The real question is: Why do we do this?

The answer may be tough to accept; it is that confusion is a luxury. You get to avoid something if you are confused. While you are throwing your hands up in the air, you get to avoid everything that you don't have the answers to. If you don't know what to do or where to start, it leaves you paralyzed. Which takes you to a place of inaction because of your confusion. Confusion typically means distrusting your own abilities and competence. And, as long as you remain confused, you never have to make a decision.

Victim Mindset 6 — Right/Wrong (Possibility) {Doom}

One of the most common victim mindsets is the need to be right. Most of the time, that means that someone else has to be wrong. This is a way to glorify your own beliefs, biases, and perspectives (sigh) and it usually means that you aren't even right—you just want the unconscious benefit of feeling that someone else is wrong. Having to be right and making others wrong robs you of enjoying the present moment because it shuts down intimacy. You can't be close to someone who is making you feel wrong all the time and if you are the one making someone else feel wrong so that you can be right, you aren't going to feel as vulnerable as you need to be. To better understand how this works, take right or wrong and replace them with the words "should" and "shouldn't." Now you probably have a better understanding of what I'm talking about.

Right or wrong stifle creativity by limiting risk-taking. If you are afraid of being labeled as wrong, how are you going to be able to feel free enough to offer a creative idea? You aren't. And this takes us to the next danger of this victim mindset: It minimizes people.

When we make people wrong, we devalue them. Their opinions, their beliefs, their very humanness all go out the window. Byron Katie put it this way: Would you rather be happy or right? Because sometimes being both isn't an option—especially when someone else has to be wrong.

What have your ideas about being right and others being wrong stopped you from enjoying?

What would happen if you came off of your position of right or wrong and just allowed things to be any other way than the way you think they should be?

One of the scariest problems that arise when we sit inside right or wrong and should and shouldn't is that there is no longer any room for facts. Facts make up the most critical part of any decision-making process because otherwise it's all opinion-based. So, when we make someone else wrong and have a need to be right, what we are really doing is ignoring the facts and buying into our own judgment.

Get out of judgment and into curiosity. Ask "Why do they do it that way? Where did they learn to do it that way? How does that make sense to them?" What would your life look like if you stopped to ask those question more, and judged the people around you a little less?

Victim Mindset 7 — Past (Freedom) {Enslavement}

Lucky number seven—the big one—is the past. A lot of times your circumstances are often very present. Rent is due in two days and you're broke. On the surface, that doesn't have a lot to do with the past. However, that's where people get caught up. They think that their current actions are based on their current belief systems. But they are not.

There is a insidious little secret lurking in the background in most of our brains. Just like Bob, the airbag-carrying man from earlier, most of us color our realities based on our past experiences. This means that we are blind to the fact that we have become accustomed to telling ourselves certain stories about how life is supposed to look.

This means that you are living in the past without even realizing it. You are using it as your reference for how your current circumstances appear. Going even deeper, the past creates a way for you to view your experiences and it may not even be factual. Instead, it is probably based on the family you were raised in and the circumstances that surrounded your childhood. A synonym for the past (psychologically speaking) is childhood. That might be a little tongue-in-cheek but it isn't far from the truth for most people you meet. This is the "thrown-ness" that Heidegger speaks about in his existential philosophy. You are thrown into this world and your circumstances and they give you a choice that can either define you and become a life sentence, or you can use them to grow and become stronger, as you would use a lesson.

When you live in the past, it's very easy to punish people for their past actions. A lot of my clients struggle with this. This book is going to challenge that by asking: "When are you going to be done punishing them?" Because they cannot be anyone else until you allow them to be someone else in your own mind first.

By staying stuck in the past, you leave no options for something new and no joy for what exists.

Keep in mind something that I tell my clients: There is no such thing as closure so I'm never going to forget that, but I have to make a choice to forgive you for that. AND every time it comes up afterward, I have to forgive you again, and forgive you again, and forgive you again.

CHAPTER TWO

Blame

B lame is the game of using other people as an excuse to give up responsibility for our actions. As an aspiring master of your circumstances, blame is the fastest way to get off course, so it only makes sense that we start there. We've all played the blame game before. *They* do this, so *I* do that. It's one of the easiest traps to fall into as a human being. And that is why blame is one of the victim mindsets that runs the deepest into our personalities.

At first, blame seems useful because it starts small. Sometimes other people will give us the benefit of the doubt when we use it for minor things. *Oh, you were late because of this external event that you couldn't control. Okay. That sounds reasonable.* But the more we use blame, the more it backfires on us. Those excuses stop working and people begin to grow weary of putting up with it. We start to shift from blaming traffic to blaming our coworkers for why we were unprepared, and this is where we begin to lose credibility in the eyes of others. The more we try to divert people's attention from our sense of responsibility, the more we look helpless, desperate, and undependable.

If you are someone who frequently blames other people, there is a very simple reason for why you do it: it works. Or, it has at least worked in the past to get you what you want. So, where does blame materialize from? Most likely, blame is a learned behavior. It becomes ingrained in our belief systems at a very young age. We hear our parents blaming the government, each other, or God for why things aren't the way they would like them to be. Because of this, blame is firmly rooted in our personalities—it is just something that we pick up subconsciously, so it impacts us on multiple levels. For instance, when we blame, we aren't really aware of our actions and we also don't have the ability to hold ourselves accountable, you know, because our excuses and reasons sound reasonable to us. Accountability gives us power, but blame will strip us of our power every time we do it. Let's dive deeper and examine the human psychology that goes into the victim mindset of blame.

Blame Broadcasts to Others to Back Off

In my own life, I liked to pass blame around a lot back in the day. I blamed my mother for the life that I was living. My mother was a single mom. I never knew my father, and every time that I asked her about him, I got a different story. Or, I got scolded for wanting to know about him, because *she* was the one I was supposed to love, not him (implied but never stated). As I grew older, I began to resent her for this and I began to blame my mother's lack of emotional maturity for my own. It was *her fault* for being cold and evasive and not teaching me how to love myself and love people.

When I got older and started dating (and even after I was married), I blamed my mom for damaging me emotionally. She was the reason I couldn't commit. She was the reason I would say the wrong thing or do something stupid. Blaming everything on my mom was a great excuse that would help me to not have to face the fact that I wasn't showing up in the ways that my partners needed. It gave me a metaphorical hall pass.

Do you remember having hall passes in school? For those of you who don't, or if you were homeschooled, let me fill you in. If you had a hall pass you were free to roam the halls to go to another classroom, the office, or someplace else during class time. This little piece of paper was all that you needed to avoid getting into trouble for being out of class. Sometimes, if you were feeling lucky, like I used to, you could go to other places and hope that the hall monitor didn't read your pass too carefully. If you didn't have a hall pass, though, the game was completely different. You were held accountable for being out of class and you were sent back to your classroom or, worse, you might even be punished.

Maybe you've used blame as a hall pass before. Chances are there are probably situations and people that you are blaming for a lot of your circumstances in life. You may not even be aware that you are doing it. In our daily lives, it can be really tempting to blame traffic or the weather for why you're late, but that isn't the type of blame that I'm talking about. While those are excuses, real blame shows up when you hold someone else accountable for your behavior. When you choose to pass blame onto another person, it lets you off the hook. It gives you the feeling that you have a hall pass—free rein to continue to avoid taking responsibility and to run around wherever you want with no repercussions. But, sooner or later, those consequences will force you to take ownership of your life.

Let's explore this a little bit more. When you start blaming other people, it helps you to look better. It is also a giant stress relief, at least at first. You put a space between yourself and your actions. You're not the one to blame, so it feels like you've solved a problem. Later on, we will discuss how right and wrong factor into this mix, because the heart of the matter is that you are really striving not to be seen as wrong or bad in the eyes of others. This is only natural and it isn't a negative thing to want to put your best foot forward. However, the real problem stems from insecurity.

Think of a person who blames their parents for why they are bad at relationships, like I did. Picture someone who is thirty-five years old blaming their mom or Dad for why they can't show up for their partner. It isn't a flattering look. In reality, what your parents did or didn't do doesn't factor into your behavior. Let's look at an example. Suppose this person doesn't like to have conversations about their feelings and lets everything build up until they explode. Imagine blaming your alcoholic father for your drinking problem. While it definitely is a factor in why you choose to do it, your dad isn't lifting the bottle up to your lips anymore. When does he stop getting blamed for how your life is going and when do you start taking responsibility for your choices?

What about the woman whose father abandoned her, so now, whenever she starts to fall in love with someone and get really close, she pulls away? She can't take the intimacy and cuts it off. She blames her father for this but it's not her father who suffers, it's her and whoever she gets close to. This is the power of blame, and this is how it can take the power out of your hands and make you susceptible to BS excuses that don't hold up. However, when you are focused on blaming, you make them seem as if they are Supreme Court-level facts. This is the danger. Have you ever been so mad at someone else for doing something that you started behaving negatively as well? They ruined Thanksgiving Dinner, so you yell and scream at them and get drunk.

Blame *never* makes sense, because normally the person blaming behaves worse than the person they are blaming. That can be a pretty tough pill to swallow. When I take stock of my own past actions, that was definitely the case for a lot of the pain and hurt that I was causing people close to me. Yes, I had been hurt by my mother and the lack of not having a father in my home, but that didn't give me the right to use that as a get-out-of-jail-free-card. There is a sensible saying, "Your freedom ends where your fist ends, and my nose begins."

So, the question is: why do we cause damage to ourselves and blame others?

You Can Never Change Someone Else's Behavior

I caution clients in my therapy practice not to want to change other people because that will lead to resentment every time. Instead of blaming other people for your actions, it is up to you to take control of your own behavior in order to feel a sense of empowerment. When you realize that you can never change or control other people, you stop blaming them. Well, at least in theory.

Behind the Blame door is the key to your hidden power. So how does not being able to change other people make you more empowered? At first, it seems somewhat counterintuitive because you have to admit that you have no control, which means you have no power over them. But tucked away in that statement is a belief. Do you see it?

It's hidden, but once you uncover it and accept that it is there, the belief will grow. The belief is this: *If I focus on what I have the power to change, I am empowered. If I focus on what is outside of my power to change, I am powerless.*

Habitual blamers will repeatedly tell you all the ways in which they are the victim. They will ramble on about how powerless they are to anyone who will listen. The more they tell this story, the more it gets reinforced for them, and the more they use it to try to elicit sympathy from others. As the title of this chapter suggests, it truly becomes a game to them. It's a game they don't even know that they're playing, though. To stay off the hook, they have to up the ante. Their problems have to get worse so they don't look bad. So long as they have more people and circumstances to blame, they never have to be accountable. Just like a drug addict, they have to get more and more for their fix. However, in the process, they begin to drive people away. No one wants to come near a blamer. Do you know why? Because they start to sound like a whining baby. Worse, they may lose their temper and start yelling at people they care about.

Blame is tricky because we start to identify with it. When we begin to base our thoughts, actions, and beliefs about how our life works around the actions of other people, we stop taking ownership.

How does this happen? We begin creating a story that strips us of all of our responsibility. You know how it goes. Here's a minor example: You are eating a nice meal with your family at a restaurant when the waiter suddenly makes a strange face in your direction. Then, the story starts to play out in your head.

Man, that guy is a real jerk, I mean we should sit somewhere else away from his tables. I guess he must be jealous that I make more money than he does. What nerve, we are paying customers. I should tell the manager!

However, the waiter's action probably had nothing to do with you at all. He may have just bit into a pepper in the kitchen or maybe the table next to you stiffed him on their tip. Whatever the case, we tend to exaggerate other people's reasons for their actions and down-play our own.

So why do we tell the story? Because we are on the defensive. In each of those examples, insecurities get activated. Blame is deeply connected to insecurity because blame is the inability to accept that maybe we haven't done everything that we needed to do to get what we wanted out of life.

Here's a more important example that will show why we do this as a defense mechanism.

Have you ever done something that you were ashamed of? I know I have. Whatever it is, you probably don't want to tell someone else about it. So long as you can keep it to yourself, it's not really that big a deal. You might feel some personal regret but, for the most part, you can handle it *or at least you think you can.* As soon as you mention it at a dinner party, though, people start to judge you. If you aren't truly okay with your actions, you will feel all sorts of shame about whatever it is that you did. If you are a blamer, you may start defending yourself. How? By blaming circumstances for why you didn't behave correctly.

At the heart of blame is difficulty with accepting reality and facing up to the fact that you didn't behave in a way that felt good to you. To transform from a blamer to someone who takes account-ability and steps into their personal power, you have to be willing to accept your actions as what you did and how you behaved. However, most people who are stuck in blame, myself included, want closure. They feel that they need some sort of magic apology that will make all the pain go away. Only then can they finally forgive the other person enough to stop blaming them.

Closure Isn't Real

I'm going to give you some really hard truth. Are you ready? The idea of closure offers a completely naive expectation that is ripe for breeding resentment. Let me explain: Most people believe in the idea of closure because it feels final. They wait for closure as a way for them to feel better about moving on. However, it is nothing more than a psychological trick to help you close old wounds and trick your mind into accepting what already is. The idea of closure can help you to move on, it really can. Here's why it isn't real, though.

As soon as you hear an old song, smell a familiar smell, or hear that person's name again, all those old wounds can rip right back open. These triggers can cause a flare-up at any time. Now, closure may not be as important as you thought it was but the real test is that when these triggers come up, you get to choose how you respond. A blamer will use those triggers as an excuse to rip those wounds right open and ruin their day. However, someone who is accountable for their actions will accept that the trigger is there and step into their real power: letting it go.

Wanting closure stems from the idea of forgiving someone for their actions. However, forgiving doesn't involve two people, it only really involves one: *you.* When you let go of the need for closure, for an apology, or for forgiveness, you open yourself up to your power. Remember, you cannot change other people, so stop trying. Even if they did apologize in the most outrageous way possible—like by buying ad space on the jumbotron at the next NHL game—it still wouldn't be good enough if you can't accept the past.

To better explain how this works in a real example, let me introduce the story of one of my former clients, let's call her Sarah. Sarah's story is a reminder that blame will never get you where you need to go.

Sarah's Story

Sarah came to me as a therapy client due to a deteriorating relationship with her husband. It was a textbook story. He would get drunk, start doing meth or whatever he could get his hands on, and engage in destructive behaviors that would wreak havoc with whatever or whoever came into his path. Usually, that was Sarah.

They had become head-locked in a vicious cycle that I see in a lot of couples: He would lose it. She would get sick of it and kick him out. He'd apologize and ask to come back and she'd take him back in again. To add to the drama, they had three kids together, so this cycle repeated over and over again until they were both exhausted.

If this was as far as it went, this story sounds pretty bad. In fact, it was pretty ugly. Luckily, it doesn't end here because Sarah realized that she couldn't do this alone. Her problems ran deep and, while he was causing most of the drama in their relationship, she was willing to accept and recognize where her responsibility in their problems came into play. This was a critical step, and it is the *only* reason why this story wasn't a total tragedy.

Sarah's problem was that she never believed in herself. Her trust in her abusive spouse had been worn down so thin that there was barely anything left. Her self-confidence had been eroded because she was constantly letting him off the hook and it drained her own belief and trust in herself. While most people would seriously consider filing for divorce, she was a product of divorce, so that was never even on the table as a viable option for her. She had seen what divorce did to her as a child and how her relationship with her dad was strained. She had seen her mother's struggle to make things work in the wake of her own failed relationship. Sarah knew that she didn't want to repeat the problems of her parents.

However, housed within this fear was an expectation (something we will get into later in this book). It was a societal expectation: *Divorce is bad.* It was reinforced by her life experience and there was no way in her mind that a divorce could end well. So what was her reward for sticking it out and making it work? Her family hated her husband, so she went into the relationship hoping to fix him and prove her family wrong. She wanted them to see how strong she was and how she could take this man who was very rough around the edges and mold him into someone her parents could be proud of—sounds pretty healthy, right? Not at all!

Instead of admitting that she failed, and getting out of the abusive relationship, she didn't want to look bad. Remember how I said earlier that one element of blame is about looking good in the eyes of others? Well, in this case, admitting that he was cheating on her, beating her, and abusing her was too difficult, not because she wanted to protect him, but because she wanted to protect her self-image. Her beliefs about who she was were so wrapped up in him that she didn't have the self-confidence to actualize herself, which is why she sought my help.

Early in our work together, she asked that he be allowed to come to our sessions. I told her that I would see them both individually. I told her to imagine that therapy is like walking along a football field and that each ten yards is a step forward. He could choose to come along and progress with us or he might be ten yards behind.

No matter what, she needed to keep walking forward to get herself ahead. Even if he was hundreds of feet behind us, she had to keep going. She agreed.

I saw the couple individually over a period of about two years. I *saw him sporadically during that period because this cycle continued*. Despite him constantly popping in and out of the picture, *she came consistently*. She did a lot of growing during that time. And, after a couple of years of committing to herself, she decided to end the marriage. This was important for her on many levels but the underlying beliefs that she had to dig up taught her that she had been relying on blame for many years. Now. the blame didn't originate with him; her relationship with him was just the circumstance that brought this out. What she realized through his example is that she needed to unpack the influence her parent's lives had had on her.

Her relationship with her parents was a recurring theme that surfaced during our work together. After a while, she began to unravel the notion that she had a strange relationship with her father. She had blamed him for dying too early. Had he not have left her, she thought things would have been different. However, we both knew that this wasn't true, because her father wasn't responsible for her behavior.

After Sarah ended her marriage, a whole new world opened up for her. She realized that she had been playing the victim by feeling trapped while taking care of her father when he was alive. She also became cognizant of the fact that she had blamed her mom for her situation. Deep down, she was harboring a resentment that her failed relationship with her dad was what led her marriage to fall apart. When she finally accepted that she was in control the whole time, she stepped into her power. She stopped blaming and her life changed as a result. Within a year, she had a better job, a man who loved her, and a healthy relationship with the past. She now celebrates her father's life and has forgiven her mom.

CHAPTER THREE

Power

*"We must also make ourselves flexible, to avoid becoming too devoted
to the plans we have formed."*
-Seneca

I hope that you are starting to see how blame is the total avoidance of responsibility. When you aren't taking care of what you need to take care of, you need to insert an excuse to let yourself off the hook. This can become a habit, and it can be a very dangerous one. It can destroy lives and ruin relationships. Blame can quickly turn into resentments that make healing very difficult.

One of the biggest things that blame communicates to the people in your life is that you are powerless over your circumstances. This can seem difficult to understand because blame is an attempt to take back control. However, it really disempowers you because it is an act of asserting that someone or something outside of your control is responsible for your actions. I know that it can be hard for my therapy clients to recognize this at first but, after it clicks for them, they make huge shifts in their lives. This chapter will show you how giving up your power through blame is a default response that is not a conscious, intentional action. Are you ready to get your power back? Keep reading. Let's go!

Be Responsible for EVERYTHING

Achieving personal power is all about taking ownership. The best way to do that is to take on as much as you possibly can. Think about successful people for a moment. Most of them work incredibly hard. They have a lot of responsibilities and they manage to perform at a high caliber, even when a lot is on the line. They don't buckle under pressure or pass the buck of responsibility to someone else. They own their power. Think back to the quote in Chapter One by Marcus Aurelius. People who master their circumstances wake up and go after the life that they want. They are driven by their dreams, not stuck in the fear of accepting responsibility.

In life, you are only responsible for one thing: *How your life turns out.* That's all. Now, that might sound funny at first because it is a pretty huge thing to be responsible for. The alternative, however, is that *someone else* is responsible for your life. This is the pathology of the blamer. Nothing is ever their fault and their life really wasn't up to them. Here's what someone who isn't in power sounds like.

Well, the President in office at the time cut my grant, so I never got to finish my degree. Had the other party been elected, I would have had the career I wanted.

You know I love music, but my Mom never let me play guitar, so I never learned how. It's too late for me to learn.

Ouch! That's painful! The alternative doesn't sound so good, does it?

While it can be difficult to take responsibility, I promise that there is a trick to it that makes it much easier. You see, life is made up of thousands of tiny choices that we must make. We all choose how to react to the circumstances in our lives. You can't change how other people react. Remember, we discussed in the last chapter how wanting to change others is the fast track to continuing to blame. So, instead, you have to make daily decisions that empower you. Now, that sounds really hard at first and it is. However, remember the alternative? Hard work is worth it, because, just like blaming, taking responsibility can also become a habit.

So the only way that this will work is if you take responsibility for *everything*. Take as much into your court as possible so that every interaction, every attitude is based on your choices and not someone else's reaction to what you do. This is where true power comes into play. If you are responsible for the way that everything goes in your life, then you are never on the defensive. You don't get offended. You don't take things personally when other people overreact to you. And you aren't bothered by someone else's behavior because you care *only* about being responsible for you. You can respond with kindness, compassion, and empathy. You can also set boundaries. The bottom line is that, no matter what kind of storm is brewing around you, you are always empowered because you get to choose your next move.

Before I go any further, here's a giant disclaimer: You aren't responsible for *how* things come into your life. You can't control traffic or the weather or how someone responds to you. What you CAN control is what you do about what happens and the attitude with which you respond. You can choose to touch someone's life with your soothing words, you can choose to be kind when no one else in the room is, and you can choose to believe that you are being set up for something better when a circumstance doesn't go your way. The secret ingredient to harnessing this power is called acceptance.

If you aren't willing to accept what is happening, then you are in resistance to what is. This is where many people start to lose their power because they can't accept what is going on in their lives. It puts them into a tailspin, because the harder they fight to resist what is, the more pain they start to feel, and then they start to take on less and less responsibility. Here's another hard truth. You may want to sit down for this one. Are you ready?

Life Is MEANINGLESS

*"To live a good life: we have the potential for it. If we can
learn to be indifferent to what makes no difference."*
-Marcus Aurelius

To anyone who studies Christianity, it seems that there is a lot of pretty clear-cut agreement as to what life is all about. However, most people overlook a pretty significant passage that I believe explains the heart of the existential question. Solomon, the man who biblically asked for the gift of wisdom, writes about how we get to derive meaning for ourselves. This example is thousands of years old, and yet it captures the very essence of personal power.

He writes:

"Meaningless! Meaningless!"
  says the Teacher.
"Utterly meaningless!
  Everything is meaningless."
3
What do people gain from all their labors?
  at which they toil under the sun?
4
Generations come and generations go,
  but the earth remains forever.
5
The sun rises and the sun sets,
  and hurries back to where it rises.
6

The wind blows to the south
    and turns to the north;
round and round it goes,
    ever returning on its course.
7
All streams flow into the sea,
    yet the sea is never full.
To the place the streams come from,
    there they return again.
8
All things are wearisome,
    more than one can say.
The eye never has enough of seeing,
    nor the ear its fill of hearing.
9
What has been will be again,
    what has been done will be done again;
    there is nothing new under the sun.
10
Is there anything of which one can say,
    "Look! This is something new"?
It was here already, long ago;
    it was here before our time.
11
No one remembers the former generations,
    and even those yet to come
will not be remembered
    by those who follow them.
-*Ecclesiastes 1*

What this means is that, when something happens it doesn't inherently mean anything in particular. For instance, how many realities are there on the planet? Can you take a guess? The answer is about eight billion.

Every person is going to take meaning differently because every person's life experience will give them a different perspective to derive meaning from. The point of what Solomon is saying is that we have to make the meaning for ourselves. No one else can do it for you. So, when we start to blame other people for why our life isn't going how we want it to, we start to give away one of the biggest and most powerful secrets on the planet: *the meaning of our life.*

Being able to make the meaning is good news for someone looking to master their circumstances. This gives us the power to view things in a positive light or a negative light, depending on the meaning that we choose. When we truly embody this power, we are then able not to take other people's actions so personally (more on that in a minute) and it frees us to do what we need to do in order to live the life that we want.

Again, this is not an easy change to make. However, when we begin to start living without judging what's happening as WRONG automatically, we start to let go of resistance. When we let go of resistance, we allow all of the wonderful opportunities that we have been waiting for to show up because we are accepting the idea that they can occur. When we are stuck in resistance, we become defensive and we are blind to what is possible.

So, what happens if something doesn't go well? We can be sad or we can change our behavior to make our circumstances better. For example, if you get in a fight with your family during the holidays, you can choose to disengage. You can peacefully leave the event and seek out a better headspace. They may get upset with you but you have the right to do what is necessary for your inner peace. You don't have to react to them trying to push your buttons. If you can accept that other people's actions have no bearing on how you choose to behave, you will be the most powerful person in the room most of the time. An important distinction to make is that this isn't about holding power over another person; that's called manipulation. This is about maintaining control over your own emotional well-being. Unhealthy people focus on the problem and focus on blame, while healthy people focus on solutions and prevention.

This is a pretty tough concept to grasp for a lot of people, so I'm going to explain it in a few different ways. If you don't understand it completely right now, don't worry. Throughout this book, I will be driving this point home in many different ways. I'm going to talk about resistance by using another word that may be more familiar: defensiveness.

Defensiveness Robs You of Power

I want to revisit the concept of defensiveness for a moment because it is such an important piece of the power puzzle. Every time you become defensive about something, you begin to lose your power. You start defending yourself by using excuses for why you aren't getting what you want. This can quickly turn into blaming someone else and avoiding responsibility for what you are doing. As soon as you act as if you are right and the other person is wrong, you've lost your power. Instead, you should try *not to react* based on their behavior. The point of this chapter is that it is *never about their behavior*. It is only about you accepting the situation so that you can start seeing clearly. When you resist *what is*, you start to fixate on how something shouldn't be the way that it is. No matter how much you try, you can't change the past. So why would you want to waste your time and energy on something you can't control?

When you get to a place of acceptance, you can see your circumstances exactly as they are. Only then can you recognize whether or not a problem exists. Only in acceptance of what is can you diagnose the problem and fix it. Otherwise, you are in resistance or defensiveness (which are really just synonyms for denial). Denial will keep you blinded to what is truly important and it can hold you back from ever facing the problems in your life that you keep avoiding.

How to Achieve Freedom:
Make Their Actions ABSOLUTELY NECESSARY

No one wants to spend their time and attention being in denial. It isn't a fun route. Being numb and blind to your pain is a recipe for disaster. The biggest problem is that you will continue to feel the same pain over and over again while trying to create new blame Band-Aids to cover it up. At some point, you have to own your problems in order to change.

One of the fastest ways to do this is through self-reflection. When you reflect on your actions, ask yourself this question: Is this within my power to change or is it outside of my power? The answer to that question tells you what you need to focus on. Doing things within your power helps you to become more self-aware and able to move forward. However, if you focus on trying to change other people or circumstances outside of your control, that is the easiest way to drain your personal power. If you can leave outside circumstances and opinions alone, there's a newfound sense of freedom waiting for you on the other side. It comes in the form of not blaming *yourself* anymore.

"It's silly to try to escape other people's faults. They are inescapable. Just try to escape your own."
-Marcus Aurelius

How someone treats you says a lot about their character. It doesn't say a whole lot about yours. The problem is that so many people *blame themselves* for how other people treat them. Just like Sarah in the case study in the last chapter: She blamed herself for her failed marriage. When she removed her own self-blaming, she stopped blaming her parents and her husband and she moved forward. Knowing how this happens can change your entire life. Using this wisdom will lead you into your power so that you don't get hung up on reacting to other people's energy.

A lot of my clients come to me in the midst of toxic relationships. They feel very codependent and as if they are powerless to change their relationships. One of the most common reasons that they feel this way is that they are stuck trying to change the other person or left complaining about their behavior. What I try to show my clients is that other people's actions are *absolutely necessary.*

Stop wishing for the other person to change. Let them be. When you can do that (easier said than done, I know) you get a sense of power in the relationship dynamic. Now, instead of trying to change the other person or fixating on all the reasons they do what they do, you can focus on accepting who they are. If you have a difficult time accepting what they are doing or you find that you can't accept their behavior, ask yourself this: Can you accept ending the relationship with that person?

You see, it was never really about that person. Just like the waiter who looked at you funny in the restaurant, your relationship is just a story that you are telling. It has always been about *you*—your reactions, your behavior, and the way you choose to let that person affect you. Here's the real magic of this chapter: When you can learn to take responsibility for how your relationships go, you can choose to make them healthy *for you*. Instead of blaming or letting other people dictate the terms, you can take the reins.

When I was younger, I looked for every chance I could to pass blame on to other people. I felt as if my life was nothing more than a series of people I needed to hold grudges against because they had somehow robbed me. Either they did something wrong to upset me (which is why I got angry) or they didn't do what I needed them to do (which is why I didn't do what I needed to in return). At every corner, I found someone else to take the blame for why I wasn't measuring up. I was constantly playing a game that was ruining my life. I was powerless to change because I couldn't admit that I was the one behind it. I didn't have the power to admit defeat. This is the real story behind someone who blames—they can't admit their faults and failures. However, the only real failure is failing to see things as they really are and not accepting them for what they are soon enough to change them. The old Jamie used to play the blame game. He loved it because it was never his fault. He didn't care how he made other people feel, it was their fault. He knew that no one can make you feel anything without your permission and he used that not to care about hurting people in the process.

The game that Jamie the therapist plays today is this: I want to leave people better than they were when I found them. So, if someone doesn't treat me right, instead of getting upset with them, I focus on how I can leave them better than they were. It takes a lot of practice to get there, but the end result has completely changed my life. I spend my time (as best as I can) looking for the 10% I can control instead of the 90% that I cannot. It just makes so much more sense. Now, when those old triggers come up with people that I had resistance to, they don't light me up as they used to. I promise you that there is nothing more powerful than seeing someone who used to fire you up not fire you up like they used to. It is absolutely life-changing. But the only way you can reach that result is if you make their actions *absolutely necessary*. Don't even take into account the fact that they could be any different, because they needed to act that way *for them*. Stop taking other people's behavior personally. Stop making their behavior about *you*.

When I am with my mom or someone who used to really drive me nuts, I don't even go down the old roads I used to. In my mind, there is a giant DO NOT ENTER sign. That exit isn't even open for me. Now, you are only human, so sometimes you will plow right through that sign, but it doesn't mean you have to keep doing it again and again. Once you are aware of the pattern, you can break it. We all have to change our dysfunctional filters and put in healthier, functional filters so that we can see our path clearly.

Use this filter: *Does this go against who I am committed to being? Does this work against what I'm building? Is this in line with my core mission, values, etc.?*

Everything you do, you get to choose. You even get to choose what it means to you. Those choices are where your power comes from. Choose wisely.

"The longer I live, the more I realize the impact of attitude on life. Attitude, to me, is more important than facts. It is more important than the past, than education, than money, than circumstances, than failures, than successes, than what other people think, say, or do. It is more important than appearance, giftedness, or skill. It will make or break a company... a church... a home. The remarkable thing is we have a choice every day regarding the attitude we embrace for that day. We cannot change our past... we cannot change the fact that people will act in a certain way. We cannot change the inevitable. The only thing we can do is play the one string we have, and that is our attitude... I am convinced that life is 10% what happens to me and 90% how I react to it. And so it is with you... we are in charge of our attitudes."
"Attitude" by Charles Swindoll

CHAPTER FOUR

Expectation

We are the result of what we think, what we do, and what we *think we should do.* We are also the result of what we *think about ourselves.* The truth behind this concept is that our perspective on who we are can shift our reality. This shift in perspective can never happen until we are ready to first accept our reality. To do that, we must be willing to dissect our beliefs and realize where they are coming from. If they are coming from our own inner guidance, we can trust them but if they are beliefs that we are holding from external expectations, we must let them go. Since our power comes from our ability to accept things as they are, it is imperative that we understand what expectations we are placing on ourselves. Only then can we enact the change we wish to see in our reality,

One reason this work is so profound is that it calls us to really identify where our strengths and weaknesses lie. This work isn't easy. It forces us to take the journey from our external frustrations with how we wish the world would be and move into our internal beliefs that are creating that frustration.

Once we see those frustrated, tired beliefs we can realize that we no longer have to identify with them. But most of us get ourselves into trouble by letting our beliefs go unchecked and then, before we know it, they turn into expectations. Let me explain what this looks like because this process usually happens subconsciously without us being aware it is even taking place. To combat this lack of awareness, we have to look for the unconscious expectations that are covertly running our lives in the background and sabotaging our future.

To understand why we are unhappy with our lives, we have to look at the beliefs that are the source of our discomfort. We must place our beliefs under a microscope and be incredibly honest with ourselves. Without this crucial interrogation of what we believe and what we dream for the future, we may feel like we are swimming in the ocean, without direction.

What scares most people is that they will have to change directions. At first, it feels difficult. My clients use words like: *impossible, hopeless, or helpless* when they describe how they feel about the realities of their lives. This doesn't have to be the case. In fact, it can be a very different experience from that. However, it requires a full and honest examination of where you are, doggy paddling and fighting the riptides, and where you would like to be, riding the waves high above the surface. You can't surf the big waves of life without being confident enough to get up on the surfboard. However, before you can ride the waves, you have to start by swimming against the current until you have enough momentum and strength to stand up and wade through the discomfort in order to ride the waves. Once you have the strength you need, you gain something invaluable: perspective. And this perspective allows you to see what is holding you back.

Your expectations in life may not seem like a big deal. But I assure you, in the above example, they are the waves that make up your life's journey. We all have expectations. Every one of us has daily expectations. At first, they start out as small thoughts, tiny ripples in the water. But then we begin to put more belief behind them as the wind picks up and gives them momentum. Before you know it, we have actual waves that are taking our lives in a particular direction.

Some of these waves are conscious and some of them are not. When you have an expectation, it is like trying to guess which way the wind will blow. It's an impossible position to put yourself in because there is never any way to make a surefire bet on which way your wind will blow. It can also be very counterintuitive to your actual agenda because it robs you of your power. An expectation is essentially making a bet that the waves will crash in a certain way. Since you can't control them, however, such a bet puts a lot of undue pressure on you. And, unfortunately, it will never play out for you exactly how you want it to. When things don't go your way, it can lead to beating yourself up or getting upset with other people in your life who really aren't even to blame.

Do you see how this chapter builds on the last one? Every time you blame someone else, you aren't taking responsibility, so in effect you give away your power. When you have expectations, you essentially put people and circumstances into a box, limiting what is possible for you. When you try to control the waves of your life, remember one thing: You can't see the entire ocean. Instead of trying to control the waves and being disappointed when things don't go exactly as you wanted them to in your limited viewpoint, you need to free yourself up to see the entire horizon. When you think like this, it makes it a little easier to trust that you can get where you want to go without having to direct the flow of the water.

The Familiar Trap

When people write about expectations, they often touch only on the effects on relationships. While it is really important not to place too many expectations on others, it is more detrimental when we place expectations on ourselves. Since you are at the center of everything that goes on in your life, other avenues need to be explored first because the consequences of expectations can be devastating if left unchecked.

What people don't realize is that they have these expectations about everything in life, from how the grocery counter clerk should treat them, to how quickly they should be able to drive to work to beat traffic, to how well they can learn new tasks—we have hidden expectations around everything.

I'd go so far as to say that *expectations are the structure and the framework for how you think your life will go.*

The Framework to How Your Brain Works

Our brains are funny instruments. They will produce amazing outputs, but only if we input the right thoughts, beliefs, and—you guessed it—*expectations.* These expectations dictate how well we will perform. They can help drive our brains toward success or repel them like a strong magnet. Either way, our brains can only do what we tell them to do. Expectations are simply beliefs that are strongly tied to our predictions about how the future will go. But there's the trick of expectation.

We think that it is based on how the future will be but it is really based on nothing more than our past data points being recycled. Our minds trick us into believing that we are computing new answers to our old problems when in reality we are just living out Einstein's definition of insanity. Here's an example.

A lot of people don't have self-confidence because they have always had mediocre results in the past. They begin to believe that they will always get mediocre results because that's what they've always got. They've never had stellar results, so why should they *expect* anything to happen differently? Taking this a step further, they begin to subconsciously create the expectation that they can't have stellar results, because they never have. Eventually, the stress of these expectations builds up because they feel so guilty about never having had good results that they beat themselves up for it.

There are two questions you need to ask if you want to know where your expectations are holding you back. Do you not have self-confidence because you always have had mediocre results? Or, do you have mediocre results because you don't have self-confidence?

That's the million-dollar question. In life, we start to expect events to go a certain way and many of us have convinced ourselves that we are afraid of the big waves, when in reality we've never even tried to ride one before.

That's the really important part about expectation that I want you to understand. If you allow yourself to keep getting stuck, you will stay stuck. If you don't change your expectations, you will keep yourself trapped in a cage that is as narrow as you make it up to be. This is a self-imposed cage that will create a vicious cycle (more on that in a minute) because it leads to you creating even more expectations subconsciously. When you are stuck in a cage, you will want to direct and control every microscopic aspect of your life from the safety of that cage.

But you are deceiving yourself because you will make decisions from that place that keep you stuck there. Do you see how insidious that is? You will literally continue to create the same old story because you *expect it to be that way!*

So, now that you understand how expectation can get in the way of you having control over your life, you can begin to take the power back. To build on the last two chapters, expectation can be a form of blame. You begin to place responsibility on how someone else will act, and then you expect them to behave in a certain way. When they don't—*boom*—blame can set in. Think about this for a moment: Without expectation, blame cannot exist. More on that later.

The Confines of Expectation

Good, hard-working people can be very successful in their careers and very driven in life, yet they may constantly find themselves getting caught up in their expectations. You can take the most talented athlete, most prominent businesswoman, or most successful student and, if they don't have a healthy handle on their expectations, it can completely undermine any sense that they are making any progress. Perfectionism is rampant in today's social media-savvy world. And comparisons to other people are even more prevalent than ever before. Everything in our world has become filtered.

More than ever before, it is essential that we stay focused on our own alignment as opposed to the expectations of others. So how can you tell if you are placing harmful expectations on yourself? Here are some examples of what someone who is harboring unrealistic expectations may sound like.

Why do I never feel good enough?
Why do I continually let myself down?
Let's examine some crippling expectations that exist in our society. If you don't go to college, you'll never be successful.
If you aren't married with kids by the time you're 35, you've failed. You need to make six figures at least in order to be happy.
If you aren't skinny (muscular) you aren't really attractive.

Do you notice a trend here? There are a lot of ifs involved. Expectations *will always have strings attached*. When you are dealing with expectations, don't be surprised if there is *fine print* at the bottom that you weren't aware of. *If* this happens, I'll be happy and *if* they do this, *then* I'll do that is the name of the expectation game.

When you feel like you aren't enough, you always should ask yourself: Where is this coming from? What is making me feel this way? Is it something that is being driven from inside myself internally? Or is it something external that I have adopted and accepted as truth that is making me feel like this?

The Big Three

While a lot of expectations can create obstacles in our lives, the big three surround *love, money, and work*.

In Chapter One, I wrote about wanting to be the next Britney Spears and how damaging that can be to your self-esteem. At twelve, it sounds pretty awesome to be a touring musician but, at twenty-two, your life may be completely different. As a child, you aren't equipped to know what the realities of your life will look like. I'd argue that, even at twenty-two, that can be a pretty tough thing to master. I used the pop star example because most people can understand how unrealistic that expectation is. However, those same people who don't expect themselves to be rock stars put unreal expectations on themselves every day in other areas. Men and women everywhere expect *perfect marriages, perfect credit scores, and yearly promotions.*

Now, here's where this gets really sticky. Are you ready? What if your career, your marriage, or your expectations about money aren't even yours? What if you are borrowing them from your parents, your siblings, or even your mentors? Yikes!

Imagine, for example, that your father is a prominent doctor. You grew up with people in your community asking you what you wanted to be when you grow up. Wanting to make your father happy, you smiled up at them and confidently said, "I want to be a doctor!"

Fast-forward twenty years: You are eating ramen noodles every night in medical school and trying to work odd jobs in between classes and clinicals just to get by, and you are probably questioning your decision. After studying medicine for the better part of a decade, you realize you don't really want to be a prominent physician like your father. You've lost the passion for it because it was never really your dream, anyway. It was your father's expectation of you and your own personal expectation to make him happy. His expectation was placed on you from a young age but, by the time you arrived at your dorm freshman year, you had completely embodied it as your personal mission.

If you were making a choice in a vacuum, you would rather learn to code or study design because you have latent passions for those subjects that you never got to express safely in your home when you were growing up. However, you've already committed so much of your life to becoming a doctor that it can be paralyzing trying to decide whether you should move forward or cut your losses. It's not just young people in school that have these expectations and struggle with trying to reroute, it's all of us.

Remember, these choices in our lives always come back to us finding our own inner resolve, not someone else's.

Don't crowdsource your life to your friends, your family, or your community. Instead, be deliberate about what you want. Imagine someone in their fifties, realizing that they've been in a loveless marriage for twenty years. Should they just throw up their hands and resign themselves to staying in it, because that's how their life ended up?

Absolutely not. You don't have to put up with things that aren't in your best interest. Rather than wishing you could make a change, sometimes you have to be brave enough to find your alignment and act on it.

One of the best indicators of whether or not you are subconsciously living out of expectations is by asking yourself if you are doing something because it is an obligation. Try something with me for a moment. Think about what it *feels like* to do something because you feel obligated. You know what I'm talking about: when you *have to do something* and you really don't want to do it.

For instance, you may not want to go to your cousin's bridal shower, or that family reunion, or one of your friend's weddings; but, if you don't, you will feel guilty. This is a perfect example of doing something out of expectation instead of doing it out of joy. If you *want* to go to a three-year-old's birthday party because it sounds fun to play with the little kids and run around the park eating cake and ice cream, that's a different story. However, if it sounds like a complete drain on your weekend to be with thirty screaming kids at noon on a Saturday, maybe you should rethink your obligations. This is obviously much easier said than done but, once you start examining where this is occurring in your life, you can start changing it. Going back to the beginning of this chapter, most of us don't even realize where we feel obligated in our lives. The real goal of this work is to learn to notice it so that you can start to change it.

Now, I can hear some of you reading this and thinking, *"But, Jamie, I have to go to my boss's nephew's bar mitzvah, he needs me there."* Well, in that case, all I can say is that it's important to question the reasons that you are doing what you are doing. You may not be able to *cancel* all of your plans but, if you feel like you need to cancel all of your plans, you probably aren't too happy in the first place. After deeper examination, you may be able to pinpoint what is really making you unhappy and use that as a jumping-off point to begin making shifts in your life.

Life Without Expectations: The Peak Performance Mindset

Here's how life can look for you when you start letting your expectations go. You will begin to trust that things will start working out for you. You will no longer expect that every minute detail of the situation has to go according to your preconceived plan. Now, an ironic thing actually happens: You start to *expect* a "Yes" and are actually surprised when you get a "No." I'll use a sports analogy to explain.

In my son's hockey tournaments, they never go into a game thinking they will lose because that expectation will cloud their thinking and they will perform poorly as a result. They go in expecting to win, expecting success, but what's important (and this is the key distinction I really want to make) is that they don't expect that they *have to win a certain way.* This is a subtle distinction that most people don't know about. It's okay to expect to win, it's okay to expect the best in your life. What gets people into trouble is the notion that they *have to do it a certain way* and that, when it doesn't happen as they expected, they stop believing that it will ever happen.

Remember, in life, you don't have to be winning all the time and in every scenario to get what you want. Even if my son's team is losing going into the final period, they can still pull out a win, because of the way that they approach the game from the get-go.

"So, are there any good expectations?"

Throughout this chapter, we've examined a lot of the ways that expectations get us into some serious trouble without us even realizing it. However, there are also positive expectations. In the next chapter, I'll explain more about how we can use our ability to choose to empower us for more fulfillment in our lives. One of the ways that we can choose more effectively is through creating good expectations. These are called *boundaries.*

Boundaries allow us to direct other people about how they can be involved in our lives in the most effective way possible. As a general rule, they give us autonomy over what we will and won't allow so that we can approach the interactions with an open mind and a receptive heart.

So what do we do to get rid of the expectations that are holding us back?

CHAPTER FIVE

Choice

I f expectations are a difficult subject for you, don't worry; you're not alone. Most of us have been led to believe that we should behave in certain ways. However, what's amazing about moving past expectations is that we don't need anyone's permission to be ourselves. Growing up, we desperately struggled to make our parents happy. We needed their approval to get the food we wanted, the clothes we wanted to wear to school, and the toys that we wanted to play with. If we didn't make them happy, we were called "bad" and then we risked not having our needs met in the way that we wanted them to be.

Dealing with Negative Expectations

Our self-image could have been damaged by our parents' negative expectations. To feel whole, we continued trying to please them by meeting their expressed and implied expectations at every turn. In a sense, we were completely helpless to do otherwise. We had little freedom of choice. This is why our teenage years could be so tumultuous for parental relationships because children are striving so hard to differentiate themselves from their *expectation makers*. You know the drill: When parents expect too much, the teen rebels to test the boundaries. This creates friction and makes it incredibly tough to separate your personal expectations from those placed on you by your parents. Think of the medical school student who wants to drop out because he realizes almost too late that he's living his father's dream and not his own.

As a child, I struggled with a toxic relationship with my mother. No matter what we did, we never seemed to see eye-to-eye. If she said it was white, I'd call it black, or at least that's what she would say. (Are you getting a sense of what our relationship looked like?) For the longest time, I felt a thin layer of guilt for not living up to her standards. Or, I'd feel a heavy sense of self-criticism for giving in to her manipulative nature. My point in sharing this is that I know I wasn't alone. We all face parental expectations from an early age that shape our self-confidence and our beliefs about what is possible for us in our lives. When we can break free from those expectations, we reclaim our power. This process is widespread and nearly universal. Think of *bat mitzvahs, quinceañeras, tribal initiations, and freshman orientations.* Cultures around the world recognize that, at some point, we have to individuate from our parents. Many parents will quote the Bible about *honoring thy mother and father*, conveniently forgetting the fact that it also says, "Do not provoke your children to anger." When I got a little older, I made an important discovery that changed not only my relationship with my mom but, more importantly, my relationship with life...forever.

I learned that most people on the planet today aren't making choices. Rather, they are making decisions based on preconceived expectations about how society works and how people should function as a result of these expectations. Here are a few examples of negative expectations that have been carried into our society's generational beliefs.

I need to have two kids.
I need to marry someone of the opposite sex.
I need to become a nurse, like my mother.
I should probably eat a healthy breakfast and three-square meals a day.
I need to work a 9-5 job to make enough money to be happy.

Accepting the status quo is a surefire way to run into resistance in your life because, left unexamined, your life will begin to look like everyone else's and nothing like what you want or need to be fulfilled. Most of us are completely unaware that we are holding ourselves back based on the expectations we have. Yet, the secret isn't a matter of getting rid of all expectations entirely because it is only rational that some expectations can help you in life. (More on that later in the book, when we discuss the correlation between guilt and responsibility.) The real magic lies in getting rid of certain expectations.

We harbor three types of expectations that we need to let go of in order to be fulfilled. These are *expectations that we are unaware of, expectations that don't fit our lives or the purpose of what we really want to do and unspoken expectations that are placed on us.*

It can be very difficult to separate yourself from these expectations. After all, you are probably throwing your hands up and asking, "How can I possibly get rid of expectations that I don't even know I have?" That's an excellent question. Are you ready for the answer?

This whole chapter is about waking up and owning your life. To do that, you have to stop making decisions on autopilot. In a few pages, I am going to teach you how to make choices instead of making decisions. This is the answer you are searching for, but first we need to look at why so many people are afraid to own their life.

Why are so many people constantly afraid of what other people think of them? It goes back to the family unit that I wrote about a moment ago. We all have been so ingrained by our families to be people-pleasers that we aren't always skilled at giving ourselves what we need. If you don't learn how to overcome this trained approach to living your life, you won't be able to make choices and you won't be able to use your newfound wings to fly.

Letting Go of the Fear of Letting People Down

When we turn off autopilot and stop making decisions, we are going to piss some people off.

Why are you driving like that? You need to use your blinker! You almost hit that pothole! Why are you driving so fast? Why are you going so slow?

Disappointing people is one of the biggest fears that can rob you of your joy. I don't have to worry about whether or not my mom is going to be pissed off at me anymore because I no longer *have the expectation* that I need to live up to *her* expectations. Here's why— *they were never hers to begin with.* She borrowed them from her mom, and her mom borrowed them from her mom, *ad infinitum.*

Either way, whether she likes it or not, I'm going to do what I want to do. Now, in your day-to-day life, friends and parents will start guilting you into doing things that you don't want to do. Or they will act as if you've made the wrong choice, based on their expectations for how you should be. Don't let them. They will try to dig their claws in and get under your skin if you are not careful. Be strong in your resolve, no matter what, and you will know more freedom than you ever have before.

Why do you have to do it differently? Why do you think you're better than us? I don't know you anymore! You aren't the person I married! Why can't you just be normal?

When you start ignoring what people say about you, it changes how you interact with them. You no longer judge them and, when they see that, they won't be as intimidated by you. In fact, they may even warm up more to you. This can take some time, of course, but, as they see you come out of hiding, they can begin to respect you for who you really are. Or they may be threatened by your new sense of freedom and not want to be around you because it intimidates them. The choice is theirs, and you are no longer governing your life based on their reactions. That's POWERFUL!

You can stop doing things that you don't want to do when you become awake, alive, and aware that you can start changing your expectations and create a different type of life for yourself. Think about it like this: Once you understand that societal expectations are just that—expectations—you no longer have to play the game.

Think about all of the money that Americans spend on Christmas presents and holiday travel every year. It is *just* an expectation that you should be home for Christmas and you should spend a lot of money on presents; after all, kids *have to get presents*, right? *Should* they? What if I want to create a new tradition? What if, for my family, Christmas means traveling to Cancun every year and spending a week on the beach playing in the sand and eating our favorite food?

When you begin to examine your expectations, it will call you to question everything in your life and you get to choose what you want it to be. For me, my biggest negative expectation from the past was the idea of what family looked like. I grew up believing in the phrase, *blood is thicker than water*. Says who? Says your family.

It took me decades to learn that being my family doesn't give you permission to treat me or my family like garbage, just because we are related by blood. I remember having to go to birthday parties for all of my family members and it was rarely fun. The expectation was that I had to be there. I was obligated even if I didn't want to be. To me, at that time in my life, there was no choice. I was powerless. I blamed them for me not having a good time and I wasn't adding anything to the party, because I was pissed off the entire time I was there. Please believe me when I say this: If you don't get along with your family and you don't want to be around them, you don't have to be. You get to *choose* who your family is.

As you let go of other people's expectations and the expectations placed on you from society, you are actually able to choose. Not because you have to but because you want to. I get to choose to be my own reason. Everything else falls into place as soon as you do that.

Decisions vs. Choices

Inside expectation is an illusion of I AM. I am either doing this, or I am doing that. It is a game of *either or, right or wrong, yes or no*. However, behind the expectation, there is always a reason for you being or doing whichever one you choose. My goal in this chapter is to show you that you don't need to hold onto the reasons because, as soon as you drop them, your decisions fall away as well. Reasons are the only things that hold any power over you. When you have a reason for doing something, you have a justification. That justification allows you to feel obligated to do something, because it is a little voice whispering in the back of your head, *"You should do this"* when, in reality, you *don't have to do it.* What would your life look like if you gave yourself the gift of not having to do things you don't want to do?

The idea is to get as close to your truth as possible.

To accomplish that, you first have to ask yourself what is really true for you? Now, I use the word "truth" because it is so popular in today's vernacular but, if that word feels morally objective for you, replace it with "alignment." "Alignment" is a better word, because when you are in alignment, you feel centered, balanced, and as if you have the power to direct your sails. While you can't control the tides of the ocean or know with any certainty where the waves will crash, you can control how you adjust your sails.

So how do you make choices? We need to go back to kindergarten for a minute because I need you to understand this principle. There are a million ways to learn to tie your shoelaces but, if you don't do it right, it will trip you up every time. To make a choice from a place of power, you have to relearn how to tie your shoes. It may feel weird and require more effort at first but I promise you that it will be worth it in the long run. To make choices in your life from a place of power, you need to define an important distinction. Most of us are doing it backward.

Most people decide to do things, whereas powerful people choose to do them. A decision is based on experiences, reasons, and preferences from your past. When you make a decision, you are letting your future be dictated by how your life has gone. You are using past knowledge to predict the future and making a decision based on that. This is why so many people stay stagnant and stuck in their lives. They aren't really empowered as individuals. Instead, they are just rehashing the same tired reasons over and over again, leading to the same decisions. So, what can we do about this? We have to take back the power of choice in order to take back autonomy over how our future will go.

Decisions Are Based on the Past, Choices Are Based on Possibility

Choices are made freely, based on possibility. Any time a reason is attached to your action, it is a decision, not a choice. So, what happens when you start living from this place of freedom from reasons? You begin not to care what people say about you. What they say and what they think doesn't factor in anymore. It may seem super-simple and even a little trite to say that if you stop caring what other people think, it will help you to live the life you want, but if you boil down 95% of the problems that hold people back in life, it comes down to caring what people think about them. If you can be free of what people say about you, you can be free from the self-judgment that comes with it. When you release your grip on your inner judge and jury, you allow yourself to make choices that are free from the constraints of people-pleasing and your whole life will change.

Here's what a decision looks like.

Why did you go with that haircut, Jamie? *Oh, well, I was researching a bunch of men's styles and decided that this matched my facial shape the best, so I decided that would probably look better than the other cuts. I wasn't really sure, but I think it turned out all right because my wife likes it.*

Hmmm... doesn't sound very confident, does it?

Compare that with an example of what a choice looks like. Why did you cut your hair like that, Jamie? *Oh, it just felt right.* Why did you decide to buy that new truck? *I liked it.*

When you want the experience of doing something, or having something, or being a certain way, you are making a choice. When you want to check off a mark on a checklist, you are making a decision. Many times, there is no reason for wanting it other than the fact that you just do. That's what I mean by letting go of reasons.

Later in this book, I will show you how, when you can say, *"I choose, I accept,"* you begin to become the master of your circumstances. Because when you accept yourself, you allow yourself to continue to choose. When you don't accept yourself, you doubt yourself, and you have to decide by borrowing other people's confidence.

Choices allow you to try new things and to explore what you don't know without fear. When you can look at yourself and your life experiences in a new way that you had no idea you could enjoy, it will help you to grow. Remember, choices are made in the present moment. Decisions are reasons for acting based on what happened in the past.

One of the unexpected benefits of doing this work is that you receive the blessing of making choices that aren't dependent on other people's expectations of you. This frees you up to direct your energy where it is needed most. Simultaneously, it allows you not to expect too much of yourself, which, as I'll discuss in the next chapter, sets you free from guilt.

Just to be clear: There is no right option, there is just the best option for you at this very moment. That could change in a second. Now it opens up a whole other question: *What would I need for that to be fulfilling?* This question allows you to feel better about your situation, your choices, and who you are as an individual.

The Vicious Cycle

In the grand scheme of things, an easy way to identify where expectation is showing up for you is by recognizing that it takes on the form of "should." They *should*, I *should*, etc. That is your indicator. If you ever feel like you *should* do something, it is a very quick insight into the fact that you feel obligated to do it!

Be careful because, if you aren't, it will become a vicious cycle. *I should be a better Christian.* Should you? There's no expectation for perfection, yet that's what starts the vicious cycle. So many of us get stuck in this endless loop of self-hatred and self-loathing. We believed somehow that we needed to be a certain way, and when we weren't it backfires on us. Our need to compare ourselves to some other version of ourselves can literally drive us crazy and keep us from taking action.

Living into someone else's expectations can cause depression and dissatisfaction in the important relationships in your life. You think, "Oh, well, this is just how I am, it's just the way things are," when, in reality, it never ever has to be that way. We don't slow down and ask, "Well, why do I believe that?" When you start unpacking that and tracing it back, you see that it was never really about you to begin with.

So, the question becomes: *Where did this expectation originate?* Because, when you can answer that, everything will be put into perspective right away. When you realize that it's your boss's expectation, or your wife's, or your neighbor's, and not your own, you can make an informed choice. Without that knowledge, you will struggle, and you will be tormented by public opinion. If you aren't able to get yourself out of that limited awareness, you will get trapped in the vicious cycle and you will beat yourself up with *shoulds*. Expectation robs you of the freedom to make concrete choices.

In the next chapter, I'm going to walk you through the way that expectations about your responsibilities lead to guilt. Then I'm going to show you what to do about it because the real magic of choice is realizing all that you could be doing if you get rid of expectation and start stepping into choice. You become free in a whole new way which can make your life so much more manageable because you will be acting on what you really want for yourself, rather than what you think you *should* want.

What else would you be doing if you weren't living in your expectations? There is so much FREEDOM in that question!

CHAPTER SIX

Guilt (Peace)

To be a *master of your circumstances*, you need to train yourself to get out of the prison known as guilt. Left unchecked, guilt will rob you of your joy faster than anything else in your life. Unlike addiction, debt, anger, resentment, or bitterness, guilt doesn't take a lot of time to accumulate in our lives. Guilt can be felt instantly. Guilt is one of the hardest victim mindsets to remove because it is so deeply rooted in our psyches that it gets firmly attached to our self-view. Rather than accepting our past actions and behaviors, guilt sticks in our minds, playing back on an endless loop like a metronome to show us where we went wrong. When we sink into feeling guilt about our past, we begin to feel shame.

Shameful feelings immediately cause us to give up our power, stop making choices, and relinquish our freedom. In essence, we lose all sense of responsibility and begin to slip into believing that we can't change. The question we will explore in this chapter is*: How do we convince ourselves that change is possible, rather than feeling that we can't change due to the crushing weight of guilt.*

Every time I think about guilt, I like to use the mental image of a heavy, lead x-ray vest. Every time you put on the weight of guilt, it weighs you down and constricts you. However, just like the x-ray vest, it serves a purpose because it also *protects you* from facing a truth that you don't want to face. In this chapter, I am going to walk you through one more step in mastering your circumstances by leading you through the process of dealing with shame, regret, and unpleasant truths about the past so that you can rid yourself of the lead vest and live your life completely unrestricted.

Guilt Comes from Remorse

Guilt is the cloak we wear that hides our light from the world. To help you understand what I mean by that, let me paint a picture for you. When you instantly feel regret over doing something, it isn't actually guilt. More appropriately, I would call that remorse. When I refer to guilt, I am not referring to remorse. Remorse is felt instantly and can help you course-correct if you live an unwanted experience. Instead, when I write about guilt, I mean compounding remorse that sticks with you over time, like peanut butter on the spoon. It takes a lot of work to get it off. While it is very common to feel guilty about an action that we aren't in alignment with, guilt is a *lingering* feeling. It operates under the surface and directs our free will in ways that cover up our personal mastery. Guilt is a constant reminder that you are a victim. When you are consumed by guilt, you believe that you are a *bad* person and that is why your circumstances are *bad*. In fact, you believe that you *deserve them*.

This will be a useful framework for reading the rest of this chapter. Remember, having remorse just means that we have a negative association with one of our past actions. It doesn't make us *good* or *bad*. These labels are entirely unhelpful. In fact, they are the very reason that shame has such staying power in our lives. When we view our choices through the lens of moral objectivity, we can only be met with one of two choices: *shame or contentment*. However, what we'll explore later in this chapter is that there is a third alternative: *peace*.

Both guilt and remorse help to give us emotional guidance for actions that we enjoy and for some of those less than savory bone-headed moves that we don't. I can't say that I am proud of being fired from more than a dozen jobs. Looking back, those weren't some of my brightest moments. However, if I felt guilty about it, it would get in the way of me doing my job today. You can't take back the past, but you also can't allow yourself to take it with you.

Guilt is essentially using the emotional burden of some past action as a justification for why you won't succeed, today. Reread that! Guilt is *rampant* in our society and it is costing many people their lives. Now, I don't mean that it is literally *killing* people, but it is taking away their peace of mind, which, in my opinion, is something that we all need to have to truly be the master of our circumstances.

"Regret changes nothing but you."
Do I regret three failed marriages? No.
Do I regret being hateful to my daughter? No.
Do I regret a poor relationship with my mother? No.
Do I regret getting fired from more jobs than I can count? No.
Do I regret resenting my father? No.
Do I regret being inauthentic when I was younger? No.

Think about it, what would it change if I regretted those things? Would it make me a better ex-husband or a better father?

Does it change *anything*?

At the end of the day, it doesn't impact my life positively at all, so why would I want to continue *punishing myself for my past mistakes?* It would only make me feel *worse* about my life and it wouldn't help me move forward.

Does guilt change what happened? Absolutely not. Does it take away the pain? No.

I don't feel any better if I beat myself up for all of the women I've cheated on over the years. All of the wasted opportunities that I let slip by don't magically come back to me if I make myself feel like dirt about not seizing them in the past.

Yet, many people believe in their guilt. They wear it like a badge of honor and they will fight to keep it. They believe that they are bad and they can prove it to you! However, when we are so blinded by the judgment of guilt, we never see the silver lining. We completely waste the lessons that our past has to teach us. And when we do that, all of the amazing things that we worked for suffer as a result.

Having guilt is like filling a vase of flowers with oil instead of water; it suffocates the progress you've made and the life you are currently living. It doesn't do anything to help you take strides forward and make changes in your life, it only keeps your hands tied behind your back, waiting to fall into the same old familiar patterns.

Guilt Is Blaming Yourself

So, what is guilt really about? When I felt guilty about my failed marriages, did I really give a crap about my ex-wives? At some level, I'd be naive to say "No." However, the main event was a big, old pity party for Jamie. *Oh, man, I screwed everything up again. I just can't believe what a screw-up I am. I will never be happy or make someone else happy. That's just the way I am.*

Guilt is all about *me. Poor, pitiful me. It is a personal feeling that sabotages your ability to see yourself in a position of power.* You instantly give up whatever sense of responsibility you have in your life when you start to give in to guilt. *Ah,* isn't it nice to feel sorry for yourself? You can wrap yourself up in a blanket and bust out the half-gallon of mint chip ice cream and watch Netflix because you *don't have to deal with the circumstances currently in your life.* Why not indulge in the old emotions of the past? That's always a safer bet because the feeling is always the same. *It sucks.*

So why do we do it?

Guilt makes you powerless because guilt is really your ego slipping through the cracks in your memory (remember how we said memory is unreliable?) As you sift through the cracks, you begin trying to cycle back through your life experiences to shift the blame away from yourself. Any time you do that, ironically enough, your power goes straight out the window, along with your self-confidence, your worthiness, and your autonomy.

You are essentially spending your time and energy talking to the walls and telling them how you were right and *so-and-so* was wrong. And get this: That's the best-case scenario! Even if you convince yourself that you really weren't the one who was wrong, you've gone straight back to *blame. Do Not Pass Go, Do Not Collect $200, Go Straight to Jail!* All you've done is to once again convince yourself that you are incapable of change. The only way you can reclaim your power is by stripping yourself of the layers of shame, embarrassment, unworthiness, and lack of dignity.

We are all familiar with the story of Little Red Riding Hood and the layers of clothes that the Big Bad Wolf wore to hide his true identity. Sounds a hell of a lot easier said than done, I know. However, the answer is surprisingly simple. If you realize that, so far, each chapter of this book has been built on the one before it, we can revisit the idea of choice.

The Power of Choice

As I shared in the last chapter, your choices will define the circumstances that come into your life. There's no denying it, there are also consequences for your actions. This is one of the fundamental principles of human existence. However, when you make a choice, rather than a decision, it gives you the freedom to take a new route, to go a new way, and to have a new experience.

When you get rid of guilt, you end up with peace. So where does guilt really come from? Guilt comes from expectations. It comes from that place that tells you that you *should* behave in a certain way.

When you own your *choices, you can't be guilty*. You can only be empowered. *Even if you didn't make the "right" choice*! Guilt robs us of our ability to express ourselves and share our purpose with the world! If you make a mistake, start thinking about it as a way that you expressed yourself, not as something that you did wrong!

Guilt Is an Expectation

Are you starting to get a sense of how all these chapters are interconnected?

Guilt is really a should. I should have done this, you should have done that, I don't know why I didn't do this. These questions never really help you. You didn't do it sooner, because you didn't do it. End of story. Place your energy in something that you can control. Otherwise, your peace of mind will be at risk.

"I should be happier!"

One of the sneakiest ways that guilt creeps into our lives doesn't happen when we are sitting on the couch thinking about exes and crying over old Facebook photos. That's not sneaky at all. We all know that guilt can make us do stupid stuff like that. However, even for a Jedi like me, there are ways that guilt slips in undetected. That is why I am writing this book, not just to share with you what I've learned, but as a reminder that this is a daily battle.

Here's how this shows up and manifests for me. The other day I'm driving in my truck. I have my big morning energy drink, I'm on my way into the office, and *bam* out of nowhere it hits me! (No, it wasn't another car) it was the realization that *I should be happier.*

Out of nowhere my happy morning suddenly got very *unhappy.* Because I wasn't happy *enough.* I was only *sort of happy,* and I felt *awful* about it for the rest of my drive. Then, as I was walking into the office, I thought, "Well, why should you be *happier*? Says who? How do you know? Why aren't you happy? Or, are you just convinced you are unhappy based on what you thought happiness was?"

When I really broke it down, it was an expectation I held that had nothing to do with my current circumstances and everything to do with where I thought I should be and how I thought I should feel. My current guilt level was through the roof, all based on a flimsy expectation that took me thirty seconds to debunk. Yet, it wreaked havoc on my day for more than thirty minutes, and it could have derailed it entirely had I not have stopped to try and *accept* my current reality. That acceptance eventually led me to find peace.

Overcoming Guilt Around Boundaries

Here's another way that guilt creeps back into our lives unde-tected: When we start to stick up for ourselves. When we honor our own integrity through creating boundaries, guilt loves to rear its ugly head to prove to us that we aren't worthy of having autonomy. No, guilt instead tries to convince us that other people's needs are much more important than our own. *"Remember that thing you did? Yeah, you aren't good enough to have boundaries," guilt likes to say.*

Even when saying "no" to someone else is a positive thing for our life, guilt can undercut the power of our choices. Guilt loves to keep us in bad situations because it lowers our sensitivity to BS. In effect, this is how it strips us of our happiness.

Doctor Henry Cloud, the writer and author of the book *Boundaries.* says this: "No is a complete sentence." There is no expla-nation needed.

If you feel compelled to explain why you are saying "No," there is more going on here. You need to examine that. It will show you what your perceived inadequacies are so that you can work on uprooting them from your life.

If you don't examine this discomfort, here's how it will show up for you. You will start believing that it is okay to feel responsible for other people's reactions and disappointments, and you will even start feeling responsible for other people's entire course of life. Recall I said earlier that guilt is all about me. You become omniscient and all-powerful because you begin taking responsibility for things that are far beyond your control. If you believe that there was something that you should or shouldn't have done or there was some way you should or shouldn't have been, you are basically saying that you had the power to control someone else's life. That is a pretty bold belief! So why do we fall into the trap of thinking we can control other people's lives?

Guilt is based on a benchmark of performance. It is often built on unconscious, unrealistic expectations. These expectations don't hold water, and they never did in the first place, which is why you *never met them*. However, in hindsight, it is so easy to look back and blame ourselves for other people's actions. Let's go back to the idea of internalized guilt, which is the guilt that we feel toward ourselves. Removing guilt is really being okay in your own skin. When I'm confident that what I'm doing is right for me, it doesn't matter what anyone else thinks, says, or does. Here's an example of how guilt can cripple a person.

You Don't Need to Relive It

History can teach us several lessons, but the beauty of history is that we don't need to relive it to extract the lesson from it.

One of my clients, let's call him Kevin, was a perfect case study for how guilt can literally wreck your life and hold you back.

Kevin had just turned twenty-one when he and his best friend went out drinking one night. They went out and they both got pretty drunk. Kevin's friend decided to get behind the wheel and persuaded Kevin to come with him. Just as Kevin was about to get in his friend's car, the girl he was with invited him to go home with her. He agreed. Less than ten minutes after they left the bar, Kevin gets a call that his friend had wrapped his car around a telephone pole and died.

In the aftermath of his friend's death, Kevin felt tremendous guilt. He blamed himself for his actions. He felt guilty that he didn't die as well. He had a nonstop barrage of questions that gave him constant anxiety. "I shouldn't have let him drive. I should have been in the car too. I should be dead. Why him and not me? Why did I let him drink that much? Why did I ask him to go out drinking that night?" They were never-ending. All these things. Then, as the family started finding out, they blamed Kevin, too. This went on for fifteen years. Fifteen years! Finally, he showed up in my practice. At this time, he was always pissed off. He has a very short temper. His marriage is a disaster and he works 80 hours a week because he feels like he has to prove to everybody that he is not a failure. He never *ever* mentions his friend's name because he will lose his cool.

At first, he was pretty upset about us even discussing it but, after we dug more deeply, I finally looked him square in the eye, smiled as sincerely as I could, and asked him, "What did you say to yourself when it happened?"

"It should have been me."

Kevin has lived with the unbearable weight of the guilt of being alive. With that type of pressure, there is no win for him. He is stuck in his guilt as long as he lives unless he can finally find the freedom of peace.

The "Why" Doesn't Matter

Kevin's story is an incredible reminder that why we do things doesn't matter. The meaning that we derive from them is all that matters. He could have been angry at his friend for driving home. He could have sworn off of alcohol that day and never touched another drop as long as he lived. He could have toured the country, speaking about the dangers of drinking and driving. Or, he could have convinced himself that women were the problem and vowed a life of celibacy and moved to a monastery in Tibet.

Please understand that I am not trying to belittle Kevin's problems; I am simply making a point that the meaning we derive from an experience is all that really matters. Two people can walk away from the same experience with vastly different takeaways. Their entire philosophy can be changed by a single event and skewed in completely different directions. This is where the power of choice really lies. The why doesn't matter. It only matters to you, and how you interpret it.

When something doesn't go right in our lives, sometimes we decide to attach a lot of meaning to it. When we do this, we make it mean something that *it doesn't have to mean*. You aren't wrong for putting a lot of stock in past experiences and making them mean something. However, you must also be able to catch when you have made something much larger than it needs to be. For instance, pretend you got cut from the team in Little League. Now, you can use that to make you a better player and try out again the next year. Or, you can hate sports. Neither one is correct, it is just what you made that experience mean in your life!

Next, we begin to start verifying whatever theme we chose to be a staple in our lives. This is where the real danger of making meaning based on guilt lies. We begin looking for reasons to say, "See, I told you so—I'm not really good enough!" So, what happens if you, like Kevin, have had an experience recently, or in the past, that made you rethink your life and create meaning where it didn't necessarily *need to belong*? The only way to get over the past is to learn to accept it.

Acceptance Leads to Peace

Remember how, in the final pages of the last chapter, I wrote that acceptance is a choice? When we choose to accept, we remove guilt, because guilt can only be present when we can't accept our choices. What happens when we can accept our choices?

All of this revolves around acceptance. A lot of life is just showing up and choosing to accept, rather than resisting what IS. When we resist, we are fooling ourselves into believing that we should have acted differently, which is a huge waste of energy that completely hinders the forward momentum of our lives.

The mindset that you need to adopt to find peace and acceptance is: It is possible that I could mess this up but, if I do it's okay, because I know I'll recover. Now, that's a power statement! I know you don't know this, but I'm a pretty big guy and, when I say that I'll recover, people tend to believe me, but I haven't always trusted myself in that way. You see, at its core, acceptance is trust. Call it faith, belief, or perseverance, but when you can trust in the optimism that the future *can possibly* be better than the past, the whole world becomes available to you. Remember, when you get rid of the regret of who you were, you get rid of the guilt for who you haven't been.

"What guilt do you have for who you haven't been?"

Do you have guilt over who you haven't been in the past? Good. Most people do. Now go be that! If you are reading this, you have time and you now have the perspective to live those desires in a way that is truer than it would have been had you done it before. Now you have the gift of insight into why you have been doing what you were, and now you can do what you need to.

This is how you gain peace in your life, by being grateful in the present moment and knowing that you can attain the life you've always wanted if you stop hiding yourself in guilt. Guilt is a secret, whereas acceptance is a flashlight. Guilt is something that you stuff away. But you are never going to get rid of the guilt until you shine a light on it and bring it out into the open.

Peace is really forgiveness. It is self-forgiveness and forgiveness for those who have wronged you. One of my clients was abused by men and she felt guilty for constantly having trouble with painful emotions when the past came up. We talked about the forgiveness that she needs and that she doesn't need to forgive them, for their conscience. Forgiveness is a tool to empower *her*, not for her abusers. Forgiving them is all for her. She struggled with bitterness and anger popping up out of nowhere. So I explained to her that what she has to get clear on is that forgiveness is an ongoing process. It's never complete. I wrote about this earlier in the book and I'll say it again in big, bold letters: **CLOSURE IS A MYTH!**

There is no such thing as a one-and-done on forgiveness. There is no such thing as lasting peace or acceptance that lasts for years and years uninhibited. These are myths.

Do I sometimes need to forgive myself for ruining multiple marriages? Yup. Do I sometimes need to reflect on how I could be a better husband, or a better father, or a better therapist? Weekly! However, that doesn't mean I've completely shut the door on the lessons that the past has taught me. Instead, I *can constantly embrace the power of owning my life experience and using it to create new experiences that are even better.*

The real beauty of acceptance is that you don't want to change the past. When you no longer care about the past, you can embrace today. This is what the philosophers meant when they said the only way out is through. You have to live your life and you have to be present enough to take it day by day and remember that doing your best is the best that you can do!

CHAPTER SEVEN

Being Overwhelmed (Control)

B y now, I hope you are beginning to see that, when you begin taking ownership of your life, that choice is accompanied by a seismic shift in your perspective. When you realize that the one common denominator in all of your circumstances is you, it starts to make it pretty difficult to wave your finger and blame other people. I want you to pause before we dive into this next chapter and take a moment to really reflect on all of the different types of circumstances that you find yourself facing. Think about what repeatedly shows up for you in your job, in your relationships, and in your response to other people and events outside of your control.

When you stop to think about it, there are probably some similarities between the problems that you had last year and the problems that you have this year. The people in your life (aka the characters) may have changed but the script is probably still very much the same. Until you change the director, the direction of the plot will never change. It's sort of like re-watching all of the Rocky movies: You know what is going to happen. After a while, even the best stories start to get old.

When you shift how the story is framed, you can take the reins on *how you choose to feel* about what goes on in your reality and what it means to you. Remember, once again, you make the meaning. Nothing in your life is good or bad, you get to choose how you feel about it. And that means *all of it.*

As you go through this journey of life, it can feel as if everything is coming at you all at once. When you stop to take a deep breath and check in with yourself, the stress and pressure that you feel every day can begin to overwhelm you physically, emotionally, and spiritually. Everyone has felt that feeling before; it's called being overwhelmed. But I bet that you didn't know that, physiologically speaking, it isn't *natural* to feel overwhelmed. Unless a giant tiger is hot on your heels chasing you through the Amazon. Our socially acceptable *responses* to technology, poor diets, and a penchant for victim mentality makes us *think it is okay to respond this way to stress.* It's not, it's just what everyone else is doing. Mastery requires you to do things differently.

Let's revisit the concept of you being the director or, since this book is about mastering your circumstances, let's refer to it as being the ringmaster of your own life. If your life is anything like what mine used to look like, calling it a circus would be a compliment because it was absolute chaos. Using that metaphor allows us to see that, even though the audience sees a circus as a polished performance, to the performers and the ringmaster, every night is like jumping through hoops, literally! Keep in mind, there are *dire* consequences to failing if you are a high-wire trapeze artist or a fire juggler. Circus performers literally put their lives on the line night after night and make it look easy, despite the death-defying obstacles they are risking their lives to perform.

I use this analogy because I want to drive home the point that *none of this work is easy.* Working on yourself while feeding your family and keeping a roof over your head is a fantastic accomplishment. Setting aside my therapist hat for a moment (and putting on my St. Louis Blues hat): From one human to another, I never want you to feel that you should have everything all worked out *all of the time.* The truth is that our society puts so much pressure and weight on us to be perfect that we often forget the struggles that we *all* must face and overcome. Just as with a lion tamer, things can go wrong at any moment. However, that can *never* be where we allow our focus to rest. If an acrobat loses her focus for a split second, she could topple to her death. Now, that's a pretty scary reality but that reality is a real possibility every day in a circus. And I'd be willing to bet that every day you pull off some impossible stunts and you probably make it look easy, too.

We all walk a tightrope that no one else will ever see. This is why I want you to be very gentle about approaching the topic of being overwhelmed because, for the most part, it is an added stress that we feel we carry alone. I want you to take a moment to acknowledge all of the triumphs you've had and the strides you have made in your life up to this point. No one else could do it exactly the way you did it. Not a single soul on the planet will ever know your exact struggles. Remember that, because it will allow you not to be so hard on yourself, which is one of the biggest contributors to being overwhelmed.

Being Overwhelmed is a Mindset

When we discuss the concept of being overwhelmed, it is important to remember that a lot of it has nothing to do with the difficulty of the tasks at hand. In reality, most of our lives are pretty manageable, we have our routines, and we can create success for ourselves. When we begin to feel gradually overwhelmed (more on that later), we quickly forget all of that structure and security; our sense of ease and flow are the first things that get chucked right out the window when faced with the impending fear of being overwhelmed. We immediately begin to stop focusing on putting one foot in front of the other and start to get upset, even bitter, about the difficulties we face. Bitterness and cynicism are among the worst impacts of being overwhelmed. But even they fail in comparison to the powerlessness that we experience in moments like these.

Don't forget that you are calling all of the shots and directing all of the performers in your reality, even though it may not feel like it. Since you are reading this book, I hope you are starting to see how, every time you begin to go into a victim mindset, it is for one singular reason: *avoiding responsibility*. At the heart of this book is the concept that you really have more control than you think you do. When I tell therapy clients this, their first response is often to freak out! I remember how I reacted when someone first told me this. I got defensive, my body language changed, my heartbeat elevated, I huffed and puffed, and then I started projecting my emotions onto them, *without even realizing I was doing it!* Nine times out of ten, we aren't aware of our role in being overwhelmed.

You see, in my reality *it had to be that way. Jamie was the victim.* Everyone else was the bad guy! If I had control over my situation, why the hell was I in this mess in the first place? Only an *idiot—an absolute moron—would screw up three marriages,* how could I be so stupid?

I had to be the one who didn't have any control. I wasn't wrong. Hell, I was the one working my tail off to get ahead. I was the one who had the difficult upbringing, growing up dirt poor. It was all about *me, me, me.* And then, when stress and outside pressure entered the picture, it shifted to being all about how I wasn't good enough, smart enough, or disciplined enough to get what I wanted.

You need that report by Monday? *What about me?* There's a red light and I'm late for work and stressed about my finances. *Crap, what about me?*

My wife is upset that I broke my promise to pick up dinner. *What. About. Me?*

Do you see how, every time something comes up, most of those that stress us out aren't even the real culprits? Yet, we treat them like they are. We think we are getting away with a fancy form of projection, but it's more like a tuxedo t-shirt—it's pretty easy to see it for what it really is: defensiveness.

As we learn to shift this mindset, away from self-centeredness and self-sabotage, it's paramount to our success that we shift our *language*. The words we use in our self-talk are crucial to how we show up in the world and how we view our current circumstances. When you think about being overwhelmed, what are some words that you use to describe it?

Drained. Exhausted. Run-down. Out of it. Slammed with work. Swamped. Impossible. A mountain to climb.

I can think of many times in my life when I have felt like my back was against the ropes. Every time, if I listen to my self-talk, I can hear it *before* I start to feel it. You can *hear it* before you *feel it.* That's what mastery looks like when you are really in tune with yourself. It is a very important concept to explore as we begin to dive deeper into the problem of being overwhelmed because the words we use have power in our lives. They give us a clue about the way we internalize the *feeling* behind them. Remember, you make the meaning. So, if you use words that mean something very negative, you begin to tack that meaning onto your experience. So, when you tune in and really listen to your self-talk, it will leave a breadcrumb trail for you to follow in order to figure out where your anxiety is coming from. If we feel like we are *slammed with work,* what we are really saying is that there is a ton of pressure on us. We feel that we are being crushed by the weight of it. More likely, it is our thoughts and what we repeatedly say to ourselves over and over again that are making us feel that pressure. Again, many times we will hear ourselves saying it before we start feeling it. This weight accumulates day after day and what started as a small snowball can turn into an avalanche. So, the question we need to ask is: *What creates being overwhelmed?*

Air Traffic Controller

A lot of people would say that a high-pressure job is the cause of being overwhelmed. However, I would argue from firsthand experience that *not being in control* is more stressful than stress is. Let's do a little experiment. Name the most stressful job that you hear about all the time. What crazy job tops the list? Bingo. You guessed it: air traffic controller.

Guess who was an air traffic controller in the Navy? Yours truly. When people learn that their therapist used to be an air traffic controller, they ask me, "Wasn't it stressful?" My answer is always the same: "No. It was great."

Air traffic control is very regimented, very highly structured. I was in the military; I was already used to that. Sure, you need to be imaginative and it is definitely an art form but, as long as you understand the rules, you will never go wrong as an air traffic controller.

Still, the noisy peanut gallery whispers, "Well, those are $80 million airplanes" or "That plane has 300 people on it, doesn't that stress you out?" I want to say this with as much sensitivity as possible. When you know how to do the job, the job is very simple. There is a complex algorithm that is just like playing a video game. After years in the military, I mastered the game. Once you get the hang of it, it doesn't drastically change. It makes a lot of sense and you get to a point where you are really good at it. All that you have to focus on is just a dash on the screen and, if I play the game by the rules, I cannot go wrong, so I control what I can control. By understanding the bubble, (every airplane has a bubble of 3 miles between aircraft and 1,000 feet above and below) where no other aircraft are permitted at any given time, it's like clockwork.

However, if you start thinking about the hundreds of lives that could be lost, or the expense of the airplane, or the *what-if* scenarios, what is really going on? It's a form of being overwhelmed and an attempt to control things outside of your control. I could never control what the pilots did or didn't do, but that wasn't my concern. So many people worry about what their boss is going to do or how their spouse will react when, in reality, it is just a way for many of us to let go of responsibility.

"You can't control that which you don't understand."

If you don't understand it, how are you going to master it? Where does being overwhelmed come in?

When you are in over your head. When you are outside of your wheelhouse. When you are trying to do something that you aren't capable of doing. When you aren't prepared to do what you need to do. When you aren't equipped to do what you have to. You will stay stuck in frustration.

When you say "I don't understand this" or "This is outside my control," leave it at that. From experience, I know that most of us say, "Well, *I know it's outside my control,*" and—get this—*Despite my knowledge that it is outside of my control, I am still trying to control it anyway!*"

Of course, you feel overwhelmed, of course, you feel frustrated— *you are trying to do the impossible and beating yourself up for it!*

Some people use being overwhelmed as a game and an excuse not to change. They know they can't do the impossible, so they use that as a rubric to judge themselves. They trick themselves into self-defeating thinking: *Well, I can't change. That's just the way I am. You don't understand, I wouldn't even know where to start.* "Being overwhelmed creates an implicit pressure in life to do or perform."

The reason that we are so *addicted* to feeling overwhelmed is that most of us who live in the Western World have become perfectionists. We are so stuck in comparing ourselves with others that we can't accept ourselves as we are. With the Internet at our fingertips, we are constantly bombarded with advertisements, social media pages, and information that tell us we should be doing *more, or that we are NOT enough.* This creates an impossible pressure to *do* or to *perform.*

So, when we examine this and break it down, we really begin to find that being overwhelmed is a negative belief about yourself. It is a lack of faith, trust, and belief in your ability to do or perform. Most often, it doesn't have a lot to do with you in the beginning. Instead, it starts as something external that you are doing that makes you feel as if you can't measure up. What I see happening in so many clients is that this feeling of being overwhelmed begins to creep in once some sort of external measuring stick comes into their lives. It could be a new responsibility at work, a new boss, a life change or transition, or something that makes them reevaluate the way they see themselves.

Then they subconsciously respond to this new thing by making their self-worth completely dependent on being able to meet all of these standards. And, in their minds, those standards are too difficult, the bar is set too high, and it feels as if, no matter what they do, they won't succeed. So they get overwhelmed and then they *allow* themselves to feel hopeless.

Out of that hopelessness comes a desperate need to *do something*, and with all of the pressure to perform it can be very difficult to know what to do so they become paralyzed, stuck in fear, confused, and even self-loathing.

Paralysis by Analysis

The average person spends a lot of time sitting worrying about one of two things: the future or the past. When you are overwhelmed, there are no good options to act on. Everything you do becomes a choice that will be wrong. There is no possible outcome that will get you what you want, so you start to overthink *everything* to support this belief. You are paralyzed by the fear of being wrong, the fear of looking stupid, the fear of failure, and the fear of public opinion. What if they judge me? What if I can't pull this off?

As a result, you are left not knowing where to start. You begin to procrastinate and you put off doing the simple things that you need so you won't feel overwhelmed. As you continue doing this, it compounds and wears on you until it finally creates a physical shutdown (which I will show you in a client example later). You've turned it over and over in your mind so many times that you are absolutely stuck.

When you don't know which way to turn and there isn't a clear answer to what you need to do first, it makes sense that you would feel overwhelmed. First, recognize that it is okay to feel this way. Acceptance is the key to understanding how you can change your reality. However, you can't stop there. Accepting it is a powerful step but it takes more to master being overwhelmed. You then have to find out where your system broke down.

Most often, being overwhelmed is not a breakdown in productivity or intelligence, as people commonly misinterpret it. It is mostly a breakdown in integrity. You lose focus because you are constantly circling around, not knowing what to do. Your loss of focus is caused by your burning up all of your energy in wondering what you should do next.

The thought pattern goes like this: Whatever I do it's not going to be enough. It's too late. How am I going to fix it now? My question to you is: "Who told you that you aren't enough?"

If you are paralyzed, you're wasting all of your energy being worried about what the right thing to do is in your situation. You spend a lot of time focusing on that, so you take *zero action*. You're completely paralyzed. You're not doing enough. Then you start to believe that you can't make anyone happy. You regret your choices and you make sure that you never repeat them...until the next time you do. For many, the pain of failing at something in the past means they will *always avoid it in the future*. It is a very subtle psychological self-sabotage, but it repeatedly shows up in people being overwhelmed. In other words, they do it to themselves, as a form of punishment for not being enough.

Being Overwhelmed Is a Sign You Don't Know Your Values

As you are scrambling to make room for all of the tasks that are overwhelming, you begin to really beat into your skull the idea that you aren't enough. Oh, look, *now I have to sacrifice my family time because I'm behind at work…again. Well, we won't take that vacation this year, because I didn't work hard enough to get that promotion.*

These thoughts start to wear down your values. You begin to feel so worthless that you stop adhering to the integrity you once had. Now, to make up for the perceived letdown of your self-esteem, you begin trying to make up for lost time. You begin feeling guilty (remember the last chapter) and then you start overpromising because you've underdelivered. Being overwhelmed is there to show us that our priorities are out of alignment. Whenever you are scrambling, you know that you have overcommitted. When we overcommit, it isn't fair to anyone else around us, but it also isn't fair to ourselves. Often, this isn't really our fault; it isn't about being *bad* or not *good enough*. It is simply that you have a conflicting set of priorities. Your highest valued priorities are conflicting with your plans or someone else's demands on your priorities. This is where the tension and frustration come in and that is what wreaks havoc in your life.

What's one of the fastest ways to drain your battery? PLEASING OTHER PEOPLE. More realistically, the culprit is *trying to guess what will make someone else happy and then compromising your integrity to make yourself fit into that box.* This is a recipe for leaving yourself completely empty.

It isn't easy, but it is always worth it.

Trying to make everyone happy is a full-time job and you waste so much energy because, no matter what you do, it won't ever be 100% right or perfect. No matter what you do! That's a big piece to remember in this puzzle. If you can accept that other people might be upset with you prioritizing yourself, then it makes being overwhelmed a little less scary and making decisions a little easier.

Many times, ridding ourselves of the burden of being overwhelmed can be as simple as asking more direct questions and searching for the answers. I sometimes swear that my job as a counselor is one of the easiest in the world. It can feel like I have to be Captain Obvious but that's just how deep some of this goes for clients. In fact, most of us are completely incapable of seeing the blocks right in front of us because they are caked on like mud that's been worn on our faces for years! You've heard, "Can't see the forest for all the trees," right? That's it, right there.

One of my clients has been married for over three decades and he was being overwhelmed because his wife wanted him to be a good husband. So I asked him: What does being a good husband mean? He just shrugged. He had *never even asked her to define what a good husband was to her*. His values were compromised because he wasn't clear what her values were. We dug a step deeper and he had also never really contemplated the question, himself. He had already chalked himself up as a failure before even playing the game.

A lot of times, when we are overwhelmed, we really need to ask for help. However, in our society, most of us are afraid of feeling stupid, silly, or weak if we seek help. One of the things that I strongly urge my clients to do is to ask themselves when they start to feel overwhelmed, "What's on my plate that I can ask for help with or delegate to someone else?"

Not asking for help and having to *prove yourself* is a recipe for being overwhelmed which will most likely just end up making the circumstances in your life a disaster. Here's why. Whenever we feel stressed, anxious, worried, or frustrated, we aren't acting out of a place of centeredness. A lot of people who are off-balance feel overwhelmed because they are not acting out of their own integrity, rather, they are trying to meet someone else's priorities for their life.

When you don't know what to do first, it is the same as being in the water and drowning; you don't know which way to turn. You don't know if you should paddle faster, paddle harder, breast-stroke wider—you don't know which way is north, east, south, or west. You are completely mixed up and you don't know how long you are going to be there. You don't know how long it's going to last, how long it's going to take for someone to find you or for you to swim your way to safety. That feeling of being overwhelmed that people typically feel – that's what the experience is like.

We get so far behind that we become desperate, careless, and sloppy. We try to prove a point to others, and we end up looking like a jerk because we never hold to our commitments. Then resentment sets in; we get mad at people for calling us out on our crap and so we dig our holes deeper. We keep digging and digging and the whole time we lie to ourselves by saying that we are digging our way out when it's really the opposite that's true. By the time we catch our breath, we are so far below where we started that our integrity isn't even an issue because mere survival is all that's left. Then we start trying to make sure we hide it from everyone we know and everything backfires. This reality makes us want to play catchup to make up for lost time, so we dig ourselves a little deeper until finally we hit our breaking point and we collapse.

Doing It All Yourself

One of my clients was overwhelmed in her life, so I started to look for the hole she was digging. Her complaint was that she was overwhelmed with everything that she had to do because she had to do it all herself. She couldn't and wouldn't ask for help. Her body reacted to this because it was overworked, too. She had anxiety, a racing heart, panic attacks, lack of sleep, physical pain, and a lot of mental exhaustion from doing everything. When we started our sessions, she would come in speaking at 400 words per minute. Then, seeing how calm I was calmed her down. There was a trust there with us. Right? That's what you do with your therapist. You have that trust. A rapport is built. It was a safe place, so she was able to just get it off of her chest. Once she slowed down, she shared why she has to do everything herself: She had been rejected by her dad.

When she was a little girl, they were best friends and her life was filled with Kodak moments. She was a pretty, pretty princess, so they had the picture-perfect relationship. Daddy smoked cigarettes and he drank a lot, but he also lifted weights. She remembers him either being at the gym or out in the garage lifting weights, smoking and drinking. Well, she went to school one day and they had a DARE assembly, where they have the DARE talk. She came home with new information about smoking and drinking that she had not been aware of before. She wanted to share that with her dad. She and her dad were best friends up until that point, mind you, so she had built up trust enough to give him information to help save his life. She was actually afraid to have the conversation because she was only eleven, so she just wrote out all of the facts on little white lined index cards and worked up the courage to stick it in his shirt pocket.

It enraged him. It pissed him off so much that he made her leave. He called her aunt, his sister, that night and she came and picked the girl up and she was gone. Later that night, her aunt and she received a phone call that he was rushed to the hospital because he had had a heart attack.

She learned that what she said and what she wanted didn't matter. That's what started her problem of being overwhelmed. She couldn't trust anyone else, because she was not worthy enough. Or she overcommitted to try to look good and avoid rejection. It was really self-punishment.

I use this client case study because being overwhelmed is a story. It is nothing more than an attempt at skirting responsibility. I just have so much to do that I can't do anything. I'm not able to control anything when I'm overwhelmed.

The only thing that you can control is what? Your attitude and your actions. That's it.

Those are the only things you can control. Nothing more, nothing less. Those are in your wheelhouse. That is the center from where you can make your integrity congruent with your behavior. It is all that is within your purview that you can handle right now. You have to give up your control of things that fall outside of that jurisdiction. Lack of boundaries and priorities will get you into more trouble than anything else in life if you let them. When saying "No" isn't okay, you've lost. When you can't say "No," there's a lack of control there. You are playing very small at that point because you have to say "Yes" to keep up the game.

CHAPTER EIGHT

Confusion (Confidence)

We've all heard the familiar joke about being in the state of Confusion as if it were one of the "Fifty nifty United States *and thirteen original col-on-ies!*" I have a son in middle school, so a few years ago I became acquainted with this little tune to help kids learn the fifty states. As you will see throughout this chapter, it's not just kids who get confused. In fact, their parents do, as well. *Oh boy, do their parents get confused!* I have majorly screwed up in my life and blamed being confused as if it was some magical crutch that could relieve me of being wrong.

For many people (myself included at times), confusion is more than just a mental state, it is an actual place where they find them-selves stuck. They have become confused and stagnant, and they have stopped advancing in their lives. While it may not be a physical location, like the joke suggests, it seems incredibly real to anyone who is claiming to be confused. This is one of those issues that on the surface can be difficult to correctly identify. Stick with me and I will show you how it probably is affecting your own life in more ways than you currently realize.

It's pretty hard to hold someone accountable if they say they are confused. It's pretty easy, on the other hand, to get someone's sym-pathy and forgiveness if we use confusion as our excuse for not being true to our word. This chapter may be tough for you to read. It may be *incredibly tough* for you if you think that you don't use confusion as a victim mindset because, the more you think that, I can almost guarantee you, *the more you do it*. Have you ever had a splinter so deep in your finger that you couldn't even see it? You can feel it, but when you go to dig it out with a pair of tweezers, you can't even begin to find it? That's a metaphor for confusion. It's there, but it's hidden so far behind the scenes that it is literally anybody's guess as to where it actually is.

If being overwhelmed is *paralysis by analysis,* then confusion can be summed up as *paralysis by inaction.* At its core, when we are confused, we claim that we don't know what to do next. It is a cleverly disguised victim mindset, hiding under the guise of a legitimate reason. You see, humans are smart creatures. Within our personalities, we have this deeply ingrained habit of wanting to look good in front of other humans. It's evolutionary. We don't want to disappoint potential mates or miss out on that big promotion, so what do we do? We lie, cheat, blame, guilt, and brag to boost our egos. Once we realize that this doesn't actually work, we sense a disturbance in the Force and have to change our strategy. This change can be pretty tricky, even if you are aware that it needs to happen. However, most of the time with confusion, like many of the other victim mindsets, you have no idea you are using it as an excuse.

If you think you are a big shot and brag all of the time about things that have never come to fruition, you will probably turn people off to whatever you are talking about. If you try to blame others all of the time, you'll notice that people don't really invest in you. If you cheat or lie, your reality will probably give you pretty clear-cut signs that you should stop doing that to protect your relationships. So why do so many of us use confusion?

Short answer: It works. Long answer: We get sympathy from people, we get extended deadlines, or we get extra help.

How is Confusion an Excuse?

That brings the question: How can someone use confusion as an excuse? Isn't it natural to be confused? I remember the first time my commanding officer in the military told me that no one else could make me feel anything. I was pretty dang confused by that statement. It took me a few days of contemplation to really grasp what he meant. That's a natural form of confusion. You don't always get things right off the bat. It took me some time and some life lessons to understand that I was in charge of not only the machinery I operated in the military but the emotional machinery that I had to maneuver to be a better man. Still confused by this distinction? Rest assured, this isn't easy wisdom. If you need a litmus test to determine if something is genuine garden variety confusion or the victim mindset, ask yourself is this something you need to learn more about? If you don't need to learn more about the situation, then you aren't really confused, you are just stalling on making a choice or decision.

On the other hand, sometimes we like to play dumb and feign ignorance. Remember what I said about humans wanting to look good in front of their peers? Well, that's what I meant. If we don't know what to do, we can't be *wrong*. (More on that in the next chapter.) As we progress and move through life, our situations change but our responses and habitual ways of being usually don't until our patterns get interrupted.

This is why I try to teach my children to recognize these things early on. For example, whenever my young son doesn't take action in school or on the ice in hockey, it is really easy for him to say that he didn't know what to do. Put differently, *he was confused.* This is really just a conditioned way to bypass our responsibility.

Here's an example. Imagine that you have a homework assignment due. You get confused and you have some questions for your teacher. The student who is truly confused *takes action* by contacting the teacher to get help. The person who wants to use it as an excuse doesn't do the assignment and, when it comes time to turn it in, feigns confusion. This is the distinction between how confusion can point us in the right direction toward obtaining more knowledge and how it can hold us back from doing what we know we need to do.

Avoiding responsibility is a nifty little trick that we learn how to do as children, which is why I like the homework example so much. We learn that if we ask enough questions, we don't need to do the work on our own. For instance, if my son eats all of the Doritos and I ask him what happened to them, there's a pretty good chance he'll quickly say that he doesn't know. "I don't know" can be an empowering statement that conveys humility if you truly don't know something but, in this case, he is saying that so that he can't be held accountable for eating all of the Doritos. Now, that's not a big deal, you might say. However, in marriages and professional relationships, this type of avoidance can get you and your partner into a lot of trouble. When communication breaks down to the point where you start saying "I don't know" it is a wake-up call that something isn't right.

So, what is the reward for all of this? You get attention. You get to play the victim. You get to avoid responsibility. And you get others to help you or even do all the work for you. In fact, confusion is a huge luxury.

I know from firsthand experience that it doesn't feel very good to hear that. However, when you are actively trying to avoid responsibility, there is virtually no limit to how far humans will go to avoid pain. Think of how pain shows up for you in your life. Now, think about what is really behind that pain? If you were to shine a light on your pain for a moment, what would its shadow look like?

Fear.

Confusion Is the Fear of Consequences

Confusion allows us to ignore our fears about a person, a circumstance, or an obligation. Nine times out of ten, we are really afraid (almost paralyzed by) the fear of consequences. This is where being overwhelmed starts, but confusion isn't the same as being overwhelmed because confusion is less defensive and more strategic. When we are afraid of the consequences, what we are really afraid of is the fear of taking the next step.

You can probably think of a friend who has created something really wonderful but won't ever publish it, sell it, or move on to the final step. This person's zip code is Confusion 90210. No matter what might happen in their life, they will always reroute everything to their new postal code because they don't want to deal with it. A new promotion comes up. Great! Send it to Confusion 90210, because I don't want to have to think about it. To take it a step further, this fear is really the fear of risk.

Humans are naturally risk-averse. We love our certainty. We like knowing that our favorite show comes on once a week, on Thursdays at 9 pm. We love our office hours and our weekends off because they give us a sense of safety. It's familiar. So, when we discuss the fear of risk, all of a sudden we lose that certainty and the identity we've built up for ourselves in that safety net.

If you want a good mental image of someone afraid of risk, think about security being a nice warm blanket (or you can even picture a nice warm glass of milk), and can't you just see that adult person all curled up with their blankie and milk, hoping that nothing ever changes?

That's a polite way of saying that, if you aren't open to change, you're a baby. Because, when you are a little child, change is really scary. However, when you are an adult, you've been through so many metamorphoses, that you're already a butterfly—so what's the big deal about having another cocoon? The answer comes back to fear of the unknown and the fear of uncertainty. What if it doesn't work out this time? What if I fail? Fear loves to focus on the *what-ifs* of life, instead of the *possibility.*

The fear of uncertainty allows us to neglect things that we really don't want to be responsible for in the first place. If you don't know what to do, why do *anything?* Another entrenched fear in all of this is the fear of time and the fear of missing out (FOMO). If you take one step left, you can't go right. It is a completely risk-averse way of thinking that limits your reality and what is possible for you.

So, what's the main goal in all of this? I'll say it again: It allows us to avoid responsibility and risk. When we are afraid of the risk or we don't want the responsibility of the risk, we just say "Well, I'm just confused."

As humans, we are so afraid of the unknown that it paralyzes us. Have you ever seen someone with stage fright? An hour before they go on stage, they are an eloquent, graceful orator, loquacious enough to make the old Bard himself feel a little. Yet, five minutes before they go on, they forget the English language and start mumbling in some form of ancient Hebrew that no one can understand, while beads of sweat start pooling on their forehead.

I want you to think about confusion differently for a moment. Imagine that confusion *is a luxury*. Imagine that, if you are really struggling in life, you don't have time to be confused, so you must be in a pretty good place if you are stalling and biding time. When we avoid something or don't know how to proceed, it is usually for one of two reasons. We don't know what questions to ask or we don't know the answers to the questions we *have asked*. Then we lose track of what is really important and begin underestimating our ability to take action in the first place. This leads us to use not knowing where to start as an excuse. So, I'll ask you this: **What do you have the luxury of avoiding?**

Confusion Is a Permission Slip

To make this really simple, let's go back to grade school again for a moment. Do you remember the colorful permission slips that they passed out to all of the students and you had to get your parents or legal guardian to sign it to authorize the school to take you on a field trip?

Confusion is a big rainbow-colored permission slip allowing you not to do anything for the foreseeable future. It happens all the time, all around the world. It's not just individuals, it also involves companies, sports teams, politicians, and just about anyone who is afraid of losing. When you are afraid of losing, you play so small that it isn't even worth you taking the chance, to begin with. And this is precisely why so many people will take a risk, give it a half-baked try, and then confirm their own self-defeating bias that it was never meant to be, to begin with.

As a hunter, I've always loved what Mel Gibson's character in *The Patriot* tells his son about shooting. "Aim small, miss small," is the family's motto. Meaning, if you aim for the head, there's a good chance your musket fire will career off the trees. But, if you aim for a stripe on the deer's coat, or a button on the Red Coat's shirt, for instance, you will still hit your target, because you are aiming for something small and precise. When you don't know which way to go, your tendency can be to become a victim and fall into the trap of confusion. We just aim at whatever comes along. However, this is when we need to be more specific, so that we can really hone in on what we want, rather than sitting in the deer stand all confused and waiting around for the sun to go down. In this famous movie scene, taking action and having a precise choice are met with a reward while aiming vaguely in a general direction with no sense of responsibility or target is met with grave consequences. Remember, both the risk of following through and the risk of not following through have consequences. Sometimes, no choice is still a choice. However, there may be another, deeper embedded fear that is really behind this lack of choice.

The Fear of Success

We're all familiar with the fear of failure. From our playground days, we know what it feels like to fall off the monkey bars in front of our crush. The sting of rejection stays with us for a long time! As a result, we are programmed not to fail. It goes so deep within the very fabric of our society that many of us are afraid to really do anything because, if we swing for the fences, we may fail. However, have you ever asked yourself what the fear of success looks like in your life? This is something that we scoff at. Isn't that prideful? Jamie has the fear of success. *Boy, that must be nice!* However, not too many of us really bother to ask the question or sit with it long enough to find answers.

When you don't know what to do or where to start, it can leave you paralyzed. This takes you to a place of inaction. You get stuck in the middle of the railroad tracks with the locomotive breathing down your neck. Your arms are bound behind you but your ties are loose enough that you can bust right through them. Instead, you just sit there panicking and wait for the train to run you over. If you got off the tracks, everything might work out but, let's face it—you've never experienced a *happily ever after* before, so why start now?

That's the fear of success showing up in your life. People fear success just as much as they do failure. It's not as simple as just sitting around waiting for the train to run you down. Instead, it's more complicated than that—I wouldn't be a good therapist if I didn't appreciate that. However, it isn't *as difficult* as most of us try to make it out to be either.

When we succeed, along with that success comes more responsibility and heightened expectations. You'll recall that, earlier in this book, I explained why expectations can be disastrous because they set us up for failure. When we have a pre-determined comfort level, we would rather sit on the railroad tracks where it is comfortable than get scraped up on the rocks by jumping out of the way. If you've ever been in a failing relationship that was toxic, you know exactly what I'm talking about. Spouses will stay in terrible relationships for *decades*. The whole time, they are completely aware of how bad it is, yet they don't want to risk something better because it is unfamiliar territory. Better the devil that we know rather than the devil that we don't know.

Confusion typically results from a distrust of your own abilities and competence. You don't leave your terrible boyfriend because you don't believe you can do better. You don't move out of your dingy old apartment because you don't feel that you deserve better. You begin to rationalize, make excuses, come up with reasons. Just as in the *Decisions Vs. Choices* chapter, this conversation comes around full circle. A good way to gauge whether or not you are making a decision or a conscious choice is by stopping and really checking in with yourself on why you are doing something. Pausing before you act allows the choice of making a wiser move on the chessboard of life. Many times, that choice is instantaneous because it isn't bound up with all of the reasons you feel obligated to do something.

It's important to check in with yourself because conscious reflection gets you out of confusion. Confusion isn't the same as contemplation any more than pacing around your house is a form of exercise. You aren't being intentional when you are confused, therefore you *aren't getting the benefit*. When you are stressed out and burning a hole in your rug with your pacing, are you really being healthy? Hell no! Your body is pumping you full of cortisol and stress hormones and you are probably reaching for a cigarette, a glass of wine, or, if you're like me, you call upon the chefs at Frito Lay to help you escape your misery—that's not exercise! If you remain confused and distracted long enough, though, the junk food companies will stay in business and you'll never have to make a decision.

Confusion Is a Call for Rescue

A lot of my clients go into therapy not really understanding where they are seeking attention in their lives. There is nothing wrong with wanting attention. It can be a very healthy human emotional need. It is when we are hungry for *any kind of attention* that we start to act out of alignment to get it that it becomes a real problem. Confusion is one of those instances. It is really a cry for help. And, even worse, it's *more dramatic than that*. Confusion is like getting a flat tire on the highway and crying on the side of the road for three hours instead of calling AAA. By the time you decide to finally dial the number, you're so worked up that you don't even resemble yourself from earlier that day. You've completely given away all of your power, probably because you had the selfish need not to *look stupid* in front of someone else. You see, confusion isn't about going to your teacher and asking for help; it's about saying you don't know so that you can give up. It is a moment of complete and utter weakness when you throw your hands up and say that you are helpless.

After all, **you can't change**.

If this book had a cheesy sitcom catchphrase like a TV show from the 1970s, I'd cue up the laugh track every time I heard someone say that they can't change because the folks at home know that everyone in the audience is about to laugh; here it is, folks, my all-time favorite psychological catchphrase—*"That's just the way I am."*

Aw, isn't that cute? Jamie is confused about being a good husband because *it's just the way he is*. So, he gets a free pass not to be in a committed relationship. He gets to play with people's feelings and let himself off the hook.

Now, someone can come to Jamie's rescue and help him feel less confused. Only, this never works out because the confusion isn't genuine, it's an avoidance tendency. And it represents a total lack of the thing that we need the most in life in order to be decisive: *confidence*.

Confidence: The Secret to Clarity

When I was selling cell phones, a mentor of mine asked me what a sale was.

I shrugged. He motioned to me with his hands, urging me to go on and give it a try. So, I gave it my best-informed guess and proudly told him that a sale was an exchange of money for a good or service.

A huge red alarm fell out of the sky and started buzzing, telling everyone within earshot how stupid I was. Just kidding, but I certainly felt dumb for being a salesman who didn't even know what a sale was. Luckily, I put aside the fear of being wrong and latched onto his words. What he said next is something that I'll never forget: He told me that a sale is nothing more than a transfer of confidence. All these years later, that has really stuck with me.

When we buy something on Amazon, we *trust* that we are going to get what we ordered. We have confidence that their complicated advertising algorithm brought us to the right product, and that the hundreds of employees working in the warehouse system will load it onto the truck, and that the pilot flying the freight plane will maneuver and finesse the plane through inclement weather so that it can land on time for a delivery driver to drop it off on the porch! Talk about believing in the unseen. Now, that is confidence! And yet, we don't give the same type of confidence to ourselves. We play into the fear of what other people want, what they are thinking, or what we perceive them to need, instead of what we need.

Confusion all boils down to a lack of confidence. It is a sale that is pending in our minds. An ellipsis is popping up on our mental credit card reader and we are waiting for ourselves to buy into our own power instead of our own crap. The dots keep flashing, but the transaction doesn't go through and those three little dots just sit there flashing, waiting for you to no longer be confused.

When you think about it this way, it seems frustrating. To the people around the confused person, it is incredibly frustrating, maybe even infuriating. Waiting to make a choice is never a powerful response.

You see, what the confused person wants more than anything is a guarantee. They want to know that if something goes wrong, *they won't be wrong.* (More on that in the next chapter.) For now, it is important to understand that what the confused person doesn't realize is that if they mess it all up, they have to trust, and trust very deeply, that they have the wherewithal to clean it up.

I've seen this time and time again in my therapy practice. Clients don't believe they can fix their lives and then Boom! Almost out of thin air, they trust the process, gain some self-confidence, and almost everything magically works out. This isn't the power of positive thinking or some #bestlife confidence hack. This is the very real power of *awareness*. What most people mistake for confidence is really awareness because it is awareness that gives you confidence. You can't have real confidence without real awareness.

One of the things that helped me to get through my flirtations with confusion was to embody the perspective that I may not know how to fix it yet but I am aware that it happened. We often go through life not even knowing that we are making mistakes and not wanting to call our awareness to the fact that they happened. To make this easier, I have a little exercise for you.

The next time you make a "mistake," I want you to remember two things. First, your best thinking got you there. It wasn't your worst thinking and it wasn't you being stupid, it was your best thinking and rationale at the moment. Then I want you to remember that a mistake is the best way to do something without understanding the full impact. You weren't being stupid; you just weren't aware of the repercussions.

Here's where our victim mindset overlooks the complete picture. Most of the time, we completely rule out our assets. We don't actually ask ourselves about the strengths that we have at our disposal.

We don't take the time to ask: What abilities do I have? What resources do I have access to that I'm not aware of or that I'm not even using? This is the biggest hurdle to real change for the confused person because they aren't even firing on all cylinders and taking advantage of what they have around them.

Confusion Is a Mask

Confidence is partly a story. I say that because it is a way to shuffle our resources around in a way that makes us comfortable. We feel comfortable about what we can do and then we feel confident. This confident self that we identify with is nothing more than a mask. In reality, we are all playing a role.

Take one of my clients, for instance. He's known as the sarcastic funny guy. Recently, after a lifetime of being the class clown and the practical joker, he started asking himself if that was really him or just his persona.

I asked him very sincerely how it was working for him. He confessed that it hurts his wife's feelings. He argued that he can't change, so I asked him what it would look like if he didn't have to be that guy?

He stared down at the floor for a few minutes before he finally said, "I don't know. I've never done it before." So, I asked him if he could do it and again he persisted, "But I'm the funny guy, that's what I'm known for. People only like me because I'm sarcastic and irreverent. I make them laugh and sometimes people think I'm pissed off all the time, but it's funny. They know it's not serious, it's just what I do."

Then, when he heard himself say that out loud, he realized that he was never that thing, to begin with, it was all an act that he was putting on to please other people. In essence, he wasn't being a genuine husband, father, or coworker, and he knew it.

If you feel like my client did that day, then I'll ask you again: How is that working out for you?

Trying on this new identity isn't easy. It takes a lot of courage to try to be better. But keep in mind that **confusion is a mask that only you see because no one else is fooled.** A lot of people in bad relationships *act* confused about what to do. Your husband is abusing you; he has been in and out of jail. You don't want to leave him even though you have to, or you don't want to be the one responsible for making that choice. It really isn't a question of not knowing what to do, it is simply: *I don't want to make a choice.* Or, I don't like what the answer is, so I'll just play dumb. Confusion is a way to get someone else to do it for you. Oh, that's fine, I'll take care of it for you. Have you ever needed to break up with someone and put it off for so long that they finally end things? That's the kind of lack of confidence I'm talking about.

Acceptance First, Clarity Second

Remember when I wrote about how acceptance is a choice? You can't choose your mother but you can accept her. Acceptance helps you to move into the present and not drag your feet. The confidence that you are resourceful and that you can overcome anything comes from accepting your circumstances. Clarity can come after you accept. Even clarity is a type of confidence because it is the confidence that you already know enough, have enough, and are enough.

So how do you get to the stage in your life where you have clarity instead of confusion? I want you to start really taking notice any time you are overcome with confusion. Really look at those patterns and ask yourself: When do I get confused? What kinds of situations have I been in recently where I feel completely confused? Start to look for the patterns and look for the kinds of things that tend to make you feel confused.

Then you can actually look at them under a microscope and discern if these are things that you don't know. Like gaps in your knowledge, gaps in your skills, gaps in your technology, gaps where your business is or where your relationships are, or if it is something you are just wanting to avoid.

That's where acceptance ties into clarity. If you don't have the guts to accept where your lack of skills lies or the courage to accept where you aren't applying the skills that you do have, you are going to be in a world of confusion. Only you can decide for yourself whether you have a true knowledge gap or whether it is just a clever ego trick to avoid responsibility.

Just as with my client the funny guy, confusion can be a mask for avoiding the unpleasantness, or the responsibilities, or the risks, or the fears or things like that. Another question that you should consider is this: "When you are feeling confused, what gets blocked out, or neglected, or pushed aside?" Those are the things you must confront to get unstuck.

The answer to these questions of self-insight will help you to peel back the mask and gain clarity over confusion. In the next chapter, I will dive into one of the most important journeys in this book: the concept of right or wrong. I explained at the beginning of this chapter that confusion is the fear of making a choice or decision that could make you look bad in the eyes of other people. If you boil that down and distill it even further, it really is a fear of *not wanting to be wrong*. Confusion is a mask that only fools you because you think it makes you right and not wrong when, in reality, it just takes away from the possibility of what you could become.

CHAPTER NINE

Right or Wrong (Possibility)

In the last chapter, I took you back to grade school. In this chapter, I'm going to show you how to unscramble some of the unconscious programming that was probably embedded into you from that period in your life. As children, we didn't get much of a say about our circumstances. In fact, much of our experience is subjective, based on our parents' and teachers' views on life. From a young age, we are taught that there are only two types of kids in the world: *good kids* and *bad kids*. Most of the time, the metric used to weigh those distinctions are the opinions of the adults you grew up with. There is no *objective* reasoning, other than the sway of their very human (and imperfect) emotions.

While great parents and teachers can make an impact that stays with us for a lifetime, even well-meaning adults can leave negative bruises on delicate childhood psyches. I know firsthand, as the child of an alcoholic, how this can affect your upbringing. Even today, there are times when I feel the aftershocks of some of my childhood trauma. What causes more psychological head trash than anything else? The concept of right or wrong.

As children, we learn that this dichotomy is the framework behind how the world works. However, with closer inspection, it really isn't based on much—if anything—other than what the adults around us consider to be right for them. The real danger here is that so many of us grow up believing that certain actions are wrong. Fast-forward thirty years and we chide our children for committing those same actions. These become deeply entrenched generational wounds that have an impact not only on how we see the world but on how our children see it, as well. This is why this concept is such a pivotal key to understanding the victim mindsets because right and wrong are the markers we use to measure our self-worth.

As adults, we tend to take on all of these judgments and embody them as our truth. As children, we are pretty impressionable. As far as ideologies are concerned, we are like a glass of water. We are bright, shiny, and clear. As the adults start pouring their thoughts and beliefs into us, it's like mixing a powder into that crystal-clear water—it gets murky and changes color and consistency. As those beliefs get stirred into us, it's pretty hard to separate the water from the mixture at first. However, if you let it sit long enough, the solid parts begin to separate from the water and sink to the bottom. This is the process that we all go through when we mature into adults. We have to separate the judgments, beliefs, and mindsets that clouded our natural judgment. However, the problem is most of us find it a lot easier to continue living in one of these outdated paradigms because it is what we know. Humans will do almost anything to look good in front of other people. However, this survival instinct doesn't really serve us when we get older. Here's a visual to help you understand how our *comfortable* and *safe* beliefs around right or wrong serve us as we age.

Imagine still wearing the clothes you wore when you were seven. Just imagine that spectacular mental picture for a moment. You're all dressed up in The Gap's finest striped button-up shirt that your mom thought would look so cute for your first-grade class photo. Your little buckle-up shoes barely fit on your toes, so you walk with a bit of a limp, trying to make sure they don't fall off. Your friends drive by on the way to dinner and notice your bright navy-blue pants are only on one leg, leaving most of your lower half as naked as the day you were born. You are certainly getting a lot of attention for your outrageous fashion sense but no one wants to be seen with you. I won't even get into the fact that no one would ever want to be in a serious relationship with you, because you aren't aware that these clothes don't even fit.

I know this sounds about as stupid as a guy wearing an airbag on his head and some of the other comical examples I've included in this book so far. However, the grim reality isn't funny at all. Many people are wearing their beliefs from when they were seven years old! They are still afraid of getting in trouble, of taking risks, or they are so self-righteous that they can't keep a partner longer than a few months. The worst part is that it is so painfully obvious to most people around them, but they have no self-awareness of it! These beliefs are so deeply embedded in us that most of the time the only way we can realize what is actually going on is through the mirror of our circumstances reflecting it back to us. For some people, that painful glance in the mirror is enough to get them to change. For others, it reinforces that they were right all along and makes them even more committed to living out a fool's errand as their life mission.

The Right Way to Load a Dishwasher

To this day it amazes me that people have some very clear and very passionate views about the *right way* to load the dishwasher. Something as simple as putting dishes in a metal cube and pushing the START button can create a world of drama and havoc for couples. It becomes a sanctimonious holy war over how to load it the "right" way—as if there is only one way to load dishes. While this seems trivial on the surface, there is a deeper layer to this, and it really sets the tone for the rest of this chapter.

Imagine that, after ten years of living with someone, you *still don't know how to load the dishwasher right.* What happens? You stop feeling valued in the relationship. Not only do we minimize people when we make them wrong, but we also devalue them. These criticisms begin to seep into more than just the soapy suds of the dishwasher. These harsh judgments begin to leak into other areas of your relationship, causing all sorts of emotional repair work to need to be done.

First, the person who is doing it *wrong* begins to feel inferior, like they are less than. Or, they become angry and will seek to assert their *rightness* in other ways. What is the impact of that? Can you be intimate with someone that you don't feel values you? Can you be intimate with someone who you believe doesn't think you are intelligent? It begins to diminish and undermine the intimacy of the relationship on all fronts. Remember, life is meaningless, so you get to choose what it means to you. In these types of power dynamics (and lording power over someone is what most of this is about), it begins to mean something much bigger than just loading the dishwasher. It starts to be a surrogate for self-worth, autonomy, and self-expression, which is serious stuff.

The person who knows the "right way" to do something is also harmed in this vicious cycle. They are setting themselves up to be disappointed based on their unrealistic expectations. Every time we want to be right, it creates an expectation that something will happen a certain way. Then it compounds because we start blaming the person who is wrong for not doing things the way we want them to. They start feeling like their efforts are unappreciated because it wasn't done a specific way. Have you ever met someone like this, who was very self-righteous? They just couldn't possibly do something about their situation. After all, they're the one who is right. Why should they change?

This type of stubborn energy creates a dichotomy of should and shouldn't. This reinforces the belief that if something is wrong you should NEVER do it. We are taught as children that we should never do the wrong thing. This can cause fear, confusion, and chaos in your life if you aren't sure what is right and what is wrong.

One of the biggest takeaways from the last chapter was the concept that sitting in confusion is caused by the fear of consequences. As children, we were afraid of getting spanked, put in timeout, or losing privileges if we did the wrong thing. We learned that doing the wrong thing had big consequences. To avoid that risk, we do nothing. When we interact with people who reinforce this right or wrong ideology (because it really is a philosophical belief system), we begin to fear making choices and acting in the world.

This can have a huge impact on your leadership abilities. These are not strictly limited to your business dealings. They extend into your work with the community as well. Everyone you interact with will feel the impact of your hesitancy. It not only limits your responsibilities, but it impacts your relationships as well. It begins to distort your filters and you begin to see other people differently. All of that only serves to keep you distant from what is possible in your future.

When you think of someone who is stuck in right or wrong dynamics, what type of person do you usually think of? Someone who is rigid, stubborn, not very open-minded or flexible. There is this underlying feeling that that person gives off to others in his or her environment that there is only one right way and it's their way.

This begins to determine how you interact with the repairman, the salesclerk, the waiter, and your children. In short, it is a stifled way of living.

If you've done something before, you think you know the right way to achieve similar results. However, what if you want to do something that you've never done before? This creates a difficult new dimension because you will find that you have limited what is right to be valid only *if you've experienced it*. If you haven't personally experienced it, then it is wrong. That makes your world pretty minuscule, doesn't it? There's a lot I don't know about in my life, so if I start limiting my personal beliefs only to things that I know, I'm going to be shutting myself off from a lot of useful information that didn't originate from my personal experience. As a result, I'm going to be a pretty narrow-minded person.

When you start pushing things off into the *you're wrong category*, you begin to lose the ability to analyze the situation effectively because you are left with only one option. However, if that doesn't turn out to be the "right" option, then you go straight back to confusion, which is why this is so dangerous. What I see in my clients is that it stifles the ability to be creative and to think strategically. It becomes a slippery slope downward until there are very few options left.

This doesn't happen just with circumstances and choices. Unfortunately, it also happens with people. Someone does things the wrong way, so we don't associate with that person anymore. It creates a very sad reality for a lot of couples, families, and friendships. Being stuck in right or wrong is one of the worst places to be emotionally because it leaves you with very little in the way of finding an answer.

Instead, it leaves you powerless, because change is very hard to instigate at this level of thinking.

The Value Is in Looking for the Answer

Remember I explained earlier that when we make someone wrong, we devalue them in our minds? The person who is wrong doesn't experience this as a projection of another person's unworthiness onto them. Let's think about this like a human instead of a therapist for a moment. If someone is telling you that you are doing something wrong, how does that make you feel? Pretty terrible. You feel like you are a failure. This person doesn't see it as a generational set of belief systems that gets passed down and projected onto them. Instead, they view it as a personal failure. They begin thinking that they need to change to fit the mold of being right. Essentially, all they failed at was fitting someone else's box. So, what can you do if you feel like you've fallen into the failure trap based on someone else's algorithm?

We need to reframe the concept of failure in terms of right or wrong. As a society, we underestimate the power of failure. Walt Disney famously said that every young person needs a good hard failure early in their career. What he meant by that, in my opinion, is that we all need a reframing early on in our life. When we "fail" at what we thought we were meant for, it helps us to learn that we are more expansive than that. We can dare to go beyond what we thought was possible in the past. When you fail at anything (from a relationship to winning the scratch-off lottery) you learn something. Look at Thomas Edison, who failed 1,000 times: He *truly believed* that he didn't fail. Instead, he found 1,000 ways not to make a lightbulb. That type of persistence is no doubt why he found success. How much value was in Edison's failures? Enough to solve the problem of the lightbulb. *That's the value.* This conversation on failure will always come back to the power of your perspective. And perspective is determined by your ability to search for new answers.

Once you start asking better questions, your framework shifts. Then you begin to feel empowered. Just like in the "Being Overwhelmed" chapter, you need to break down your goals into manageable chunks. Then, and only then, can you start reframing your life so that it makes sense to you. If you've "failed" on paper, you have to keep going anyway, so why not adopt an attitude that will help you to get out of that feeling of failure? So, what's the beauty of looking for the question? When you start asking small questions, you find other questions to ask that can lead you to where you want to be. And, as a result of that search, you begin to find other answers, too. Some of them are small pieces of the puzzle but others are integral to your success. This is how you shift your attitude. You start small and work up to a bigger mindset shift. It isn't usually an overnight process but it can be because sometimes one tiny realization is all that it takes to change the trajectory of your entire life.

The old character that I was playing was not interested in any of this mindset talk. Instead, it was much easier for the old Jamie to just blame other people. They're wrong, I'm right. It was a pretty simple story, and he didn't lose much sleep at night worrying about it. However, every now and then, he would feel a tinge of remorse, that maybe—just maybe—he wasn't living his life right. Eventually, my lightbulb moment came when I was sitting in my friend's truck and I decided to try something new because I realized that *what I had been doing was no longer working.* I had nothing to lose by trying something different. That's valuable information. That's open-mindedness. That's what I like to call *being in the inquiry*.

So how can we be more like Edison and less like old Jamie?

Being in the Inquiry

A good buddy of mine and I were talking about dating one day when I was much younger. He told me that *girls love being asked questions.* Based on his own personal Casanova tactics, he advised that I ask more questions in my attempts to *woo* the love of my life. Back in those days, I was obsessed with the conquest because it gave me a sense of importance, but I didn't understand what he meant in the advice that he gave me.

Today, it makes a lot of sense. We all like being asked questions because questions *invite* answers. He was basically telling me that I needed to take an interest in the people I wanted to date and really listen to them. As a therapist, I tell my clients that *when someone tells you who they are, believe them.* If you don't, you may spend a lot of time and headaches trying to please people who can't be pleased or worse, change people who don't want to change.

When you start asking questions about something, you begin to get into the inquiry mindset. It's not any different than a college student who loves her classes so much that she starts reading every book she can on her campus library on her favorite subjects, even though it isn't required. That journey of inquiry will lead to a simultaneous journey of self-discovery, which can lead to growth. When you are in the inquiry, you are searching for understanding, even though you don't understand it yet.

One of the most important understandings you can walk away with after reading this book is that What You Focus on Will Fill Your Field of Vision. When you are in the inquiry, you are looking at something that is open and unresolved and can be useful to you. If you already know everything and you are right, your view becomes very narrow.

To help you get a visual image of what this looks like in life, imagine you are standing at a shooting range. What do you see? You are standing there with the rifle down at your side. You see the grass, the sky, everything. You see what's around the target, above the target, and below the target. You see it all. You have a lot of perspective. You are aware of anything that comes in. However, if you lift the rifle and you look through the scope, now you just see the target. That fills your field of vision, and everything in your life experience begins to reflect that.

That's how life is.

It's not just the simple answer that you want to look for. It is seeing everything else that is around the target, in front of the target, and underneath the target. The answer is rarely *just* the thing you think you need. Instead, you need to go into the inquiry so that you can see all of the things you've never even considered. The only way to accomplish this is to ask more questions in order to find the answers you never knew you were looking for.

What would your life look like if you started doing that? Where would you go? Who would you meet? What new experiences could you have?

The Right Way to Cut the Grass

Along with this binary of right or wrong comes the judgment of other people, which can be very detrimental to your progress. Judgment never gets anyone to change; it only harms the person doing the judging because it limits their reality of what is possible in their life. Outside of morality, I personally don't believe that there is a right or wrong. There are simply, just possible ways of being. How many people are on the planet? Take that number and that's how many right ways there are to live a life as a human being. I tell all of my clients that because, when that sinks in, it is life-saving wisdom. Here's a metaphor that will hopefully drive home this point.

Think of all of the rules that come with cutting the grass. What's the right way to cut the grass? Oh, you call it *mowing* the grass... *okay*. Well, how do you mow the grass? Do you do diagonals or vertical strips? But when do you do the trimming, first or last? Do you have a bag lawnmower or do you blow your grass? You probably already have a lot of preformed ideas about the *right way* to get the job done. However, someone else from a different family probably grew up doing it very differently.

Now imagine that you are driving down the road. On a separate street, an entire team of workers is cutting the grass. One of them is blowing it off the road and leaving it all over the sidewalk. Another worker is mowing diagonally, while his coworker is mowing horizontally at the same time, and they almost run into each other when they meet in the middle. You slow down a little to watch this spectacle play out. *What on Earth are these guys doing?* You think to yourself. You start to laugh because over in the corner you have one guy out there using a mower that is at least 50 years old! What a joke! You start to drive away but then you slam on the brakes. Right in front of you is a guy crawling on his hands and knees cutting every single blade of grass with scissors. Wow! You think you've seen it all. You just shake your head dismissively as you turn back around to drive away and there, in the middle of the road, you see a guy leading a goat tied on a leash, who is literally chomping away mouthfuls of grass!

What's your reaction to this madness?

Those guys are idiots! That's wrong. They are doing it so wrong. How can anyone be that stupid?

It comes back to the central belief: *That's not the way I do it.* If we want to judge anything, there is only one metric we should use to judge something by: its effectiveness. Here's a question that changed my life to put this into perspective. *What's the right way to be a mom?*

Ouch. That one really stumped me, at first. I wanted to say, loving, supporting, or nurturing. However, the reality is that that isn't how my mom did it. So, I spent a good chunk of my life making her wrong for her way of being my mother.

I made her wrong. She wasn't wrong, I made her that way in my mind, based on what I believed was the right way to mother a son. But when I became curious about why she did it that way, it opened me up to be able to say, "You know, that's not how I would have done it, but that's just her way, she wasn't trying to hurt me." My mom was not out to make my life miserable. She could have given me up for adoption. She could have aborted me but she didn't.

This type of thinking is pretty difficult. I know from experience that it can be a hard pill to swallow at first. However, this is what allows us to give space for people to be themselves in their own way. What's the right way to be a father? What's the right way to be a girlfriend, a pastor, a friend?

This is not talking about relationships; this is just dealing with how we interact with other human beings. When we enter into a relationship, we still have to be in the inquiry in the larger scheme of things. In my life, my mom instilled in me a sense of identity in that I was going to graduate from high school. I was not dropping out.

A lot of the goal of life for me was just to make it through high school. She would constantly tell me, *Once you graduate then you get to be in charge of yourself, but until then, you are going to graduate high school.* Her job was complete. I always had food on the table. I always had a place to sleep. I always had clothes to wear.

That being said, living with my mother was difficult. It was not a sunny afternoon stroll or a fun family picnic in the park. I didn't have a great time. But, in her mind, she gave me everything I needed. And, in many ways, she really did. Without her, I wouldn't be a therapist. Without those tough experiences, I wouldn't be as good at my job as I am. That's where her head is and, now that I see that, I can relate to her. I wouldn't cut the grass that way but, hey, it's how she chose to do it.

Based on effectiveness, if I want to judge my mom, I have to judge her as being effective based on where I am in my life today as a result. She gets a pass. She didn't fail, because I am not a failure. That's the power of this chapter. It can strip away decades of blame, guilt, and anger. Just like that.

Effectiveness Is Only to Judge Yourself

When problems arise in life, if you stay in the inquiry and just focus on whether a given situation is "working," or "not working," it makes things a lot easier and cuts out the excess drama. Keeping it simple helps there to be less of a communication breakdown by getting lost in semantics. In life, things either work or they don't. If you need proof, look at professional athletes. Some of them have atrocious form but they are freaks of nature and can outperform other players who have the best technique on the planet.

We get stuck in right or wrong so much that we forget what works and what doesn't work. If the dishwasher still runs, and the dishes get cleaned, who cares how it's done? Now, I am not being flippant here, I'm just being pragmatic. I don't believe that all ends justify the means or any other extreme notion like that. As a tool, it can be very useful to see if something works before getting into right or wrong and jumping into blaming someone. If we can get into the inquiry and understand why something works or doesn't, it frees us up to stop playing politics and start judging things on effectiveness alone.

Now, not everyone is going to be comfortable with every decision other people make. For instance, if you drive at the speed limit or below, you probably wouldn't like riding with someone who goes 10 or 15 miles above the speed limit on the highway. It would really freak you out and make you anxious. So sometimes, my way is all that I'm comfortable with, and that's okay, too. Now, I know that it sounds a little contradictory, so let me explain.

My way just gets into this world of "will it work?" or "does it work for me?" This isn't negative. Sometimes, that's the best we've got. Yet, we can communicate that and say that I am only comfortable doing it this way for the time being. That's maturity. Saying that you are struggling to unload the dishwasher because you don't know where everything goes organizationally, is different than telling your spouse that they are doing it wrong and starting petty arguments. Being in the inquiry invites a conversation. As a human, you are entitled to want things to be done your way and sometimes you need them to be done your way. Some writers blare really loud music while they write. Stephen King is constantly cranking out the tunes. But other writers wait until the stillness of the night and write by candle-light in perfect quiet. What works for one author might not work for another author.

Is it working, or is it not?

Stepping into the Possibility

It isn't an easy pill to swallow, but we need to stop judging people. However, to do that, we really need to understand the *why* behind other people's belief systems. Now, I've already alluded to the fact that there are generational triggers that come into play in the right or wrong debacle. No discussion on generational wounds is complete without compassion. Compassion allows us to stop making people wrong. It also allows us to stay in the inquiry and it will give us the necessary strength to come up with new creative explanations, instead of clinging to what's familiar, which is making people wrong so that we can be right.

Here's a story that I absolutely love. A husband and wife were arguing about how to make the Christmas ham. The wife every year would cut the ends off of both sides of the ham and put it in the roasting pan. And the husband said, "Why do you do that? In my opinion, it allows the juices to seep out and makes the ham dry."

She shot back, "Absolutely not. My grandmother taught my mother who taught me. This is the way that you roast a ham. It turns out wonderful and delicious every single time. It is a time-tested way of cooking the ham." They are bickering back and forth. She calls her grandmother and tells her, "grandma, will you please tell him why it is so important to cut the ends off of the ham." And her grandmother says, "The reason I always cut the ends off of the ham was that, when we were first married and I was given all of these roasting pans, the hams were always too big to fit in the pan because our family grew so quickly. So I always cut the ends off so it would fit into the pan so I could get it into the oven."

This is a prime example of how the question of right or wrong always comes with a hidden list of expectations. This was supposedly the right way, the only way, the best way, the smartest way, the gourmet way to cook a Christmas ham, yet it was simply a practical step that had no bearing on making the ham taste better. It simply "worked" for the grandmother.

This gets into the heart of this chapter because it reminds us that, in life, we are faced with possibilities. Reality is always experience-based and a lot of times emotion-based and reaction-based. When we sit inside of right or wrong and should or shouldn't, there is no room for the facts, which are really the most critical piece of any sort of decision-making. In the above example, the fact was that the ham didn't need to be cut and, only when the facts were presented, did any real understanding occur. However, up until that point, there was no confrontation with the facts, no inquiry.

Outside of morality, there is social right or wrong that we can agree on like murder, lying, and so forth. Beyond that, there really is no right or wrong way to do anything. There are only possible ways of being.

What would happen if you came off of your position of right or wrong and just allowed things to be any other way than the way you think they should be?

Creating with Curiosity

If we want to reach people, if we want to love people, if we want to really connect with other human beings, we have to get out of judgment and into curiosity. When I'm in judgment, I'm angry. I'm cut off from the rest of existence and I'm separated from myself. Think about the creative process for a moment. Right now, you are reading something that is the result of hundreds of hours of writing, reading, rewriting, and contemplating. When you create, you don't create something that is right or wrong. There's no way to judge it. Sure, there are peer reviews and award shows for art. But, in its most primordial sense, art transcends those hardline distinctions. You just create. You decide to make something out of nothing, and you do it. There are infinite possibilities for how it could be, but you created it the way that you did. It was the right way. Creation gives you that possibility.

However, to really create, you not have to only be in the inquiry, you have to stay curious through the difficulties of creation. It isn't easy to paint the Sistine Chapel but, if you stay curious long enough, it can be done. If you lose interest, get bored, or think it isn't right, there's no way you are going to be able to create a masterpiece—on canvas or in your life.

Life doesn't come with an eraser but you don't have to feel wrong about your past. In the general sense, creation doesn't make mistakes. Everything you've done in your life so far is a lesson in perspective, a lesson in possibility, and the colors in the palette that you can use to create your masterpiece. In the next chapter, we dive into some deep water, all the way to the bottom of our victimhood. In the murky water of our past, we begin to see the possibility of what our life could be, instead of what it *could have* been.

Are you ready to take the plunge into your past?

CHAPTER TEN

The Past

What is the biggest fear on Earth? Most people would say public speaking. As someone who loves to speak in front of an audience, I disagree. However, even though I can't side with most people about what scares me the most, I can definitively say that the scariest thing on the planet isn't public speaking. It's facing your past. Coincidentally enough, facing that fear is the only way to become free in a deep and meaningful way as a human being, as a partner, as a friend, or even as a son or daughter. Until you dare to make that journey, you will always be met with recurrent patterns and reminders of the pain of your past.

Circumstances are the foundation for this book because they are the foundation of your life experiences. As we've journeyed through each of the victim mindsets, we've seen how different layers of victimhood are written into the very fabric of our life story. Our experiences weave themselves into our personality and become the basis for what we share with the world. Most of us wear our circumstances like the clothes on our back. For many people, their personality is nothing more than them showing off their past scars to protect themselves. This is a very common psychological defense mechanism that many employ. It seems like a good idea but it never actually works. When someone is owned by their past, it gives a warped misperception. They are not able to be fully genuine in how they show up in their lives because the past has its hold over them. In fact, I would argue that, in my experience as a therapist, this is what most people struggle with.

In a nutshell, mastering your circumstances is about not allowing your *past* circumstances to define you. Instead, to really master your circumstances, your duty is to reclaim them and to take ownership of them. How do you own your past? You must take back the power over the *narrative of your life*. This is how you earn your freedom from the past. I say "earn" because this is no easy task. It isn't for the faint of heart. This is why the past has such a tight hold over so many people. It takes courage to overcome the fear of the past. The past is that monster lurking in your closet or hiding under the bed. The fear of it being there is what is scary. In my own life, I found that most of my monsters were actually friendly. But this realization came only after staring into the darkness in my closet. Shrouded in secrecy, the past is an endless void of missed opportunities, regrets, and failures. On top of all of that, the past is the basis for all of our insecurities (more on this later). Our past creates the experiences that make us feel less than, defeated, and doubtful about who we are.

The failures of the past can make us feel unworthy. Why? Because we aren't perfect, and we are never going to be perfect. As Kierkegaard said, "life must be lived forwards, but it can only be understood backwards." The past is tricky, don't be fooled.

The Trick of the Past

When you bring your past into your present, you forget that your past circumstances don't exist in the present the same way they existed back then. Back then, those were your present circumstances. You reacted the way you did based on all of the evidence you had at the time. As I explained in the last chapter, your best thinking got you there.

Looking back on your life, it is very easy to see the puzzle pieces that you weren't able to put together before. This is the trick of the past: We begin to fool ourselves into believing that we knew what to do, even though we really didn't.

To put it reductively: The past is gone. It's over, baby! When you bring it back into the present, you get to color it a different way. You get to apply the rose-colored glasses and make it look all pretty. Glossing over the painful aspects of the past, or heightening those painful elements for dramatic effect, is the danger of this trick. We think that it is what "really happened to us" but our minds are wonderful shapeshifters—twisting everything around to feed our own self-serving needs for how the past can fuel our emotions. The past can either be villainized and make you feel sad or it can be glorified and make you long to go back. It is a dangerous drug that many use to anesthetize themselves to the pain of the present so regularly that they become addicted to it.

In the classic song "Hotel California" by The Eagles, the lyrics "some dance to remember, some dance to forget," are a haunting forewarning about people who are trapped in the past. But the past does have a purpose and an important place in our lives.

The Past Is a Tool for Growth

The past can be a powerful tool. It can be a life lesson or it can be a life sentence. However, just like all of the other victim mindsets in this book, it can also be a formidable self-destructive weapon. The past brings up a lot of questions. A lot of them are uncomfortable. Many of them are almost *impossible* to answer because of the combination of new information mixed with unreliable memories. These questions, when used in an empowering way, can propel you into a brighter future. You don't want to make the same choices, so you begin to interrogate yourself until you find a new and better way. The past will always hold lessons for you that you can learn at a later time. Allow that thought to sink in for a moment. Focus on the reality of that for your life. The past always holds lessons for you that can be learned at a later time. That is the ownership I'm referring to. Your past can be a lesson that you needed to have so that you can learn from it years later when you need it. If you allow yourself to choose to approach the past as a tool, you can learn a great deal about yourself, and significantly speed up your mastery over your circumstances.

However, sometimes, living in the past is nothing more than a major distraction to avoid the present; I call this taking a stroll down Memory Lane, which I'll explain later. If the present is too disorienting, we can be very attracted to living in the fantasy world of the past. We begin to make up our reality, based not on what has meaning to us in our current situation but on how painful past circumstances were for us. Like the Wizard character in *The Wizard of Oz*, we can use the illusion of the past to create a false sense of self that keeps us safe, hidden away from public scrutiny with smoke and mirrors.

Alternatively, the past can also bring us clarity. The gift that the past gives us is a perfect way of thinking about how we internally create meaning in our lives. The past is a mirror for how reality works in a world that has no meaning. Our interpretation of reality comes from an experience or a thought that we had. Sometimes, those thoughts are really just a past reaction or something that has already occurred that we are bringing into the present and then forecasting into our future by allowing it to perpetuate.

Living in the past can cause depression. Living in the future can cause anxiety. Live for the present. Live for the here and now.

The Secret to Living in the Moment

It sounds great to live in the here and now but, as you probably already know, it can be pretty darn difficult. Try telling someone who has just had their heart broken, replaying every scene in their mind on repeat, to just stay in the moment. That's naturally going to piss my client off and it will do much more harm than good because, as soon as I tell them to stop thinking about it, all of the sudden, they start to focus on it. Like a highlight reel of bad luck, the past causes us to stop looking at what's in front of us, and project our past failures into our current present. The past may trick us into getting out of the present moment. However, there is a proven way to get back into the moment anytime you catch yourself strolling down the yellow brick road of Memory Lane or replaying vicious cycles of *I should have done this, or I should have done that.*

That tool is called *intentionality.*

To live in the here and now, you must be very intentional about what you do. Think about it: If you are living in the past, you are probably regretting something, wishing you hadn't said something or thinking about all of the ways you didn't do the right thing. Is that a powerful approach to living your life and making decisions? Or is it a very passive way to avoid the responsibility of what you can control? As I explained about being overwhelmed, it is simply an excuse. Nothing more.

Mastering the past is all about being intentional and choosing to live an intentional life by creating intentional thoughts and being vigilant about where your mind goes. You can either be the passenger to where your mind is going, like riding shotgun in the passenger's seat, strapped in and along for the ride, or you can be in the driver's seat with full autonomy over how your life pans out. The choice is up to you.

Keep in mind that intentionality is not a decision. Going back a few chapters, intentionality is the *choice* that feels good and is in alignment with what you most want. Often, when we go back through our actions and examine why we did certain things that we later regret, it is because we made a decision based on facts or what *we thought we should do*, as opposed to what we really wanted. Living with intention is about having the responsibility to purposefully choose what you want in your life. Most people just sit in the driver's seat and let their past dictate everything about where they are going. However, when you are intentional, you are making a firm choice toward the outcome that you want.

The reason that I can say with such certainty that the past is so predictable as one of the biggest fears in the entire world is that the real problem of the past is forgiveness. And forgiveness is frightening. *It is also beautiful.*

Forgiveness Isn't a One-Time Thing

When I am working with a new couple in my therapy practice, they always want to talk about trust. One partner broke the trust. The other suffers from a lack of trust. They are both working on rebuilding their trust. It's always one of the first things I hear. When my clients inevitably start turning to the past to bring up examples of their partner's bad behavior, I cut them off immediately and I ask them to define forgiveness.

Then I look at these two hurting people sitting in my office and I remind them that this ethereal, magical, all-powerful forgiveness isn't a one-time thing. It isn't a magical wish, as if you rub a lamp so the Forgiveness Genie pops out and makes all of your resentment, guilt, blame, control issues, and anger go away. *Forgiveness is a way of being that lasts.*

This is the power hidden within the painful realms of the past. It is yours to seek out and only yours to find for yourself. If you don't master it, that lack of forgiveness will always be following you waiting around the next corner to pounce on you and pickpocket your joy. However, if you've mastered your past, then you have freedom and there is nothing that the past can take from you. You are whole. Complete. You have an entirely new way of being, which, as you'll see by the end of this chapter, grants you your very well-earned freedom.

I've already shared the concept that there is no such thing as closure. You are never going to forget what happened but you do have to make a choice to forgive what happened. This is a choice, not a decision. This is not something you can fake. Fake forgiveness is a big problem because it serves no one. Wearing a false veneer of happiness at church on Sunday or when you go into town, only to be miserable when you go home each night, serves no one.

Every time this topic, whatever it is, comes up again, you have to forgive again, and again, and again. This is why I want to reframe forgiveness as a way of being. It is a way of life in much the same way as being kind is a way of life for some people.

If someone has broken your trust, when you decide to get back into a relationship with that person, you have to make the conscious effort to forgive them and remind yourself that you forgave them already. When tempers flare back up, as they inevitably will, your mind will instantly say, *I don't trust you.* Then you have to grab the steering wheel and say with intention, *I want to trust you, I will trust you, I do trust you.*

On the other side of it, trust is a choice. When the past comes up, you have to treat it like it is a fossil. *Sure, it happened, but that isn't who I am today. Yes, that happened but that doesn't define me today.* A fossil is dead, it doesn't have any bearing on anything. It marks a moment in time that occurred but there isn't anything changeable to that fossil. It's just a rock. One of my clients told me that, when they were getting sober, their sponsor told them, *it's not the journey of a thousand miles that's the hard part, it's removing the rock from your shoe.* When you learn how to stop defining yourself by your past failures, you become a whole lot lighter. Where does this lightness come from?

It stems from the realization that, every time you have a painful reminder about the past, that you are *not* who you were. Today, you are not a victim of your circumstances because every day we have the gift of choosing how we narrate our reality. Just because you were someone else yesterday doesn't automatically disqualify you from being someone else tomorrow. And it doesn't stop you from being someone else right now. It's really just a battle between your ears that you can win with resolve and intention. With enough intention, you can forgive again and again. With enough resolve, you can become a different person.

When asked about winning so many golf championships, Arnold Palmer stated, "The most important 6 inches on the course is the 6 inches between your ears." He understood how important mindset is.

Forgiveness Is a Habitual Way of Being

So, how can you become intentional about overriding the pain of the past, while having the resolve to stick to it? As a therapist, I love when clients get hung up on seemingly *big problems* because it allows me the opportunity to help shift their mindset and show them how easy it is for them to change. If you have a big problem, try to find something else to compare it to, something that is a small problem. I'm not downplaying weight loss as an easy thing but, if you think of the formula to lose weight, it doesn't take a rocket scientist to figure out how to *start* losing weight. Think about it: If you want to lose weight, you replace your unhealthy habits of eating junk food with healthy eating habits. If the past is dragging you down, you have to change your habits around what you think and how you feel.

The problem with the past is that we have a habit of holding onto grudges and holding onto pain. This is just how we have been conditioned to react in our society. It may be someone who wronged you or a self-reflection of a time when you let yourself down. When I say that forgiveness is not something we do naturally as humans, it is because we love to feel bad about things that hurt us. It's another wonderful protective feature of the human brain. Naturally, if you share one news story of murder and one of everyone in town getting a free puppy, the one murder has more of an impact. It's meant to keep us safe from harm. However, this negativity is no match for a conscious forgiveness practice. The knee-jerk reaction is occurring right now but you can train yourself to have an intentional response by practicing it. Every time you have a knee-jerk reaction, like reaching for the Doritos, you can remember that you are doing something different and choose a new behavior. Staying perpetually in the moment and forgiving someone over and over at the moment until there is no need any longer for that forgiveness *is a viable option*. Well, that sounds crazy, Jamie; I have to forgive them over and over in my head? That sounds insane. People would think I was a crazy person. I hate to break it to you, but if you feel like forgiveness is hard work, look at what most people do—look at what I used to do. I used to walk around with so much guilt, anger, and regret that I would be walking down the street and having arguments with my mom, my boss, my ex-wife, my old friends, my new friends, my landlord, the cashier at the gas station—everyone and everything about the past drove me crazy. I was constantly, replaying those old dramas and making myself feel terrible the whole time, step by step, thought by thought.

We create that habit and then it just becomes who we are. It becomes second nature. Any person who has been hurt, which is about 8 billion people on our planet, will have these negative reinforcements show up. If they have been hurt in the past, it shows up in every relationship they are involved in, I promise you, because they are waiting for it to happen again. This is so critical to understanding why the past is so important and why, without learning about the past, the rest of this book will never be able to help you.

The Past Is Perpetual

When you are living in the past, you are living in perpetual suffering, perpetual guilt, and perpetual punishment for what didn't work in the past. A past-based lifestyle leaves no options and no joy. Everything is very painful. This pain blocks any new incoming information from being allowed into your experience. If you are spending all of your time focused on the past, you lose your joy because there is no discovery. There is no room for it! In fact, there is no room for anything new.

Your place in life is all based on past facts or past evidence that you have for how things are, for how people are, for how it's going to go, for how it's going to be, for what you deserve and what you don't deserve. Everything is all pre-determined; your free will is gone.

Again, instead of the possibilities that we have discussed in other chapters, you are left with no options because that's the way that it's bound to be. You already know best about what you need to do. At this point, you see things only one way. I refer to this as an unbending perspective. Your perspective is focused on the evidence that you have and your commitment to keeping things on par with the status quo.

This becomes very detrimental because you begin to assume that the way things *were* is the way they *are*. You begin to get into that confusion, which can paralyze you. Inaction and inflexibility to change overwhelm you and then you begin to blame your past self for the damage that he or she caused. Do you see how all of this works together? An unbending perspective leaves little room to grow. It leaves no room for forgiveness. It leaves no room for joy and fulfillment.

Memory Lane

Living in the past is an avoidance of the present and it is a form of escapism. That's not a popular opinion but it is true. Past-based living is an avoidance technique that tries to keep things familiar so that fear doesn't creep in but, as long as the present isn't changing, your past will strip you of your joy, time and time again.

I've already explained how, as humans, we don't want things to change. That's our biggest fear but the game that we love to play to give ourselves that sense of normalcy is called *Memory Lane*. When we go for a stroll down *Memory Lane*, we get to feel all the familiar feelings, smell all the familiar smells, and remember our life as a picturesque scene. The problem is that we've already been there and, instead of constructing a future, we are reconstructing the set of our past experiences and expending a lot of energy to do so.

Thinking of the past is like a Hollywood studio remaking the same old movie because it will sell. There's no fun, no imagination, no possibility of something better coming in. When we are so fixated on how things used to be, then what do we strive for? We strive to recreate *how things used to be*. This is another aspect of the *unbending perspective*. We then create a story about our past in our memories that probably is about as true as an episode of *Seinfeld*. Most of the time, the past is a fictional thing that we are either blatantly misremembering or are still confused about.

There is a special distinction that I want you to always, always remember. If you only remember one thing from this book, let this be it: *What happened in the past is not the same as what you made it mean.*

The meaning is how we architect the stories that become our past. Each one of them is a story that conflates the facts of what happened, with your fictitious, made-up meaning.

We begin inserting the old reruns of "*Wasn't it great when? and, Oh boy, do you remember when things were this way?*" You have to consciously recognize that you are never going to be the same person you were. We are either growing and moving forward (there is no such thing as maintaining) or we are treading water and moving backward. There is no middle ground. There is no stagnation because even stagnation is a backward way of being. It's moving back, not going in a direction of growth. Another thing that I wrote down that goes right along with this is, "The past is already done." We can't change it. There is nothing we can do to fix how things went. There is nothing. It's done. Now if we made a mess, we have a responsibility to clean that mess up. However, it's done. So, the regret that goes with it—*the I wish I would have, and I could have, and I should have*—all that does is keep us stuck in the past and stuck in regret. That is what causes depression. Because we get stuck in the "less than" right?

When we talk about the past already being done and regretting it, the beauty of the past is that everything that we did—the good, the bad, the ugly, the fantastic—has brought us to where we are, right here and right now. All of our knowledge. All of our experiences. It's the butterfly effect in action. Just one small butterfly flapping its wings is enough to cause an earthquake somewhere else in the world because it sets off a chain of events that cannot be undone. However, you can never go back because it took *all of you* to be who you are today. Every decision is a flap of that butterfly's wings; there's no way to undo it. If you want to improve on what you did in the past, you need those lessons in your arsenal to enact change today. You can't have Memory Lane without some sort of knowledge gained. It's impossible. The past is not detrimental unless we use it as such. As I wrote earlier, it can be a powerful tool or a self-destructive weapon. It can be a whipping stick we use as a measurement to show how we don't compare to other people or it can be a shield of fear that we use to keep people and possibilities from coming into our lives or it can be a lesson or a life sentence, the choice is yours.

Stop Using the Past as Evidence Against Yourself

I had a phone call with a friend the other day. It lasted three grueling hours. I was doing some work in the yard and moving some heavy stones and he was rambling on so fast that I'm sure he didn't take the time to notice. He was going on and on about a failed relationship and how he missed his opportunity a year ago! A full 12 months later, he was going on and on, replaying every scene in vivid detail. I sipped some iced tea and muted myself while he went on and on. Throughout the call, I kept reminding him that he could use this as momentum. I say momentum because knowing what you don't want or what didn't work is incredibly helpful knowledge.

As I said in the last chapter, Edison didn't fail a thousand times, he just eliminated a thousand ways that the light bulb didn't work. At one point, it clicked in my head and I realized that he was using the past as *evidence* against himself. It had been a year but my friend was still continuing to replay the court scene, over and over and over in his head. We are the judge, we are the jury, and we are the executioner. We are all of that. But the funny thing is that my friend didn't realize that *once we stop being just one of those things* it all goes away.

The trial is over. Think about it: In this simple illustration, the judge just listens to the evidence the jury deliberates on and the executioner just carries out what the judge demands. So, if we stop listening to that part of our brain that wants to stay stuck based on the sins of the past, we don't have to judge ourselves. And, once we stop judging ourselves, our chains no longer exist. We like to think that the past is in the past but it's really not. The past is the lens that we view our future through. The whole time we are using the past as a lens, what are we actually looking at? We are using it as a means for watching out for potential hazards.

Is the Past Controlling You?...
And You Don't Even Realize It?

At this point in the book, you should know that almost everything comes down to these six little words. *This is just how I am.* People who are afraid of their past take on this unbending perspective. This avoidance can be very painful, but once again it is a protective measure.

They protect themselves by feeling more powerful by blaming others for what happened in the past. They have unrealistic expectations about what they should or shouldn't have done and aren't free to make choices as a result. They choose to make others feel guilty, robbing themselves of the peace that freedom from the past can bring. They allow themselves to get overwhelmed based on the past stories that continue to perpetuate in their life. They let confusion run their confidence out the door and they live in a bleak fantasy world filled with the memories of the past. Or they choose to make others wrong so that they can feel a sense of justified moral superiority by calling themselves right. All of these approaches protect us from having to deal with the past. But what most people never consciously realize is that these are the very things that make them victims.

Typically, when the past controls us in a negative way, there is a hurt associated with it. So ask yourself what specifically hurts? Once you identify that, you can dig a little deeper and identify how this painful experience led you to believe what you currently believe. I know I have this conversation with every client in my practice. When we talk about the past, a lot of clients bristle. They don't want to dive in that deep because they have a hard time understanding that their past is what is influencing their situation today. It takes a little while for them to assimilate that information and really get it. It might take a couple of sessions for them to come in and say, "You know what? I was driving down the road and it hit me. I get what you were saying now about how my past is controlling me."

When someone is stuck, they assert that they've "always been this way." I always ask my clients, "Can you remember a time not being that way?"

We try to protect ourselves by using the past as a shield. One way that we do this is by using sweeping generalizations. If you are in a relationship with someone who causes you pain, you make generalized statements to try to rationalize that hurt. Oh, well *all* blondes act that way. Oh, *all men* are pigs. I'll never date a salesman again. I'll never trust a *waitress* again. Do you hear how silly that sounds? And yet, on an unconscious level, we do this all the time.

How does this impact how you interact with people when you are living in the past? What is your greatest relationship in life? It is your relationship with yourself. Next, of course, are the people around us. If you look at our businesses, our friendships, our families, it all boils down to relationships. That's the bread and butter of our life. When we live our lives based on past experiences, past decisions, and past judgments, that's how we decide whether other people or we ourselves are right or wrong. It's also how we decide whether they are guilty or not. Taking it a step deeper, it is how we decide whether they are worthy enough even to be in our lives, to even be in a relationship with us. The past is a huge card to be dealt. It is the dealbreaker in life. So, to have the dexterity of autonomous relationships, we need the flexibility of mind to be free from the past. More specifically, freedom from the restraints of the past.

It's not that we don't want to respect the perspective of the past but, when we are looking forward, when we are forward-focused, when we are staying in the present, sometimes that perspective needs to be malleable. It needs to have fresh edges so that it can serve us best, rather than holding us hostage.

In our relationships, **if we are stuck in our past, we keep everyone else there with us.** That's the power of the past. That is why every single chapter in this book relates back to this one principle. If we have to relive it, they have to relive it. All of our relationships stay stagnant as a result. There is no healing in living in the past. None whatsoever. Masters of Circumstance carve out their own paths by owning their past mistakes enough to use them to create a better current reality.

Acceptance is a choice. Can you accept your freedom from the past?

CHAPTER ELEVEN

Freedom

Freedom cannot be bought, it cannot be earned, and it definitely isn't something that someone else can give to you. Freedom is a power that you must claim for yourself. This is a concept that is very difficult for me to teach because it is an internal allowing that makes this possible. However, I can share with you the best attempt from my own personal journey.

All sorts of things will happen to you in your life. You'll find yourself at your wits' end trying to solve the puzzle. If you are stuck in expectation, guilt, or blame, you'll never see the forest for the trees. If you are clinging to the past as a protective blanket or wielding being overwhelmed as a shield against the inevitability of change, the opportunities that are just on the other side of that fear will never find you. The truth is, we all have only a finite amount of time on this Earth. Since you're taking the time to read this book, you recognize that. You have a reverence for life and for the people who make your life worth living. Loved ones get sick. People die. Lives are uprooted. The global pandemic reminded us all that human life is sacred. As we spend our lives trying to do a little better each day, it's important to remember what is truly at stake: our hearts.

True freedom isn't about having material wealth or a fulfilling career as the American dream has promised us it would. Instead, real freedom can be found only in the intangibles. When our minds are free, we can act in the world. We can have success. We can achieve our goals. But when our hearts are free, our spirit is free to connect with everyone who crosses our path. In that freedom we find love and in love we find our truest selves. I don't just mean romantic love; I mean unbridled love that is unrestricted and not limited to a textbook definition.

Remember how earlier in this book I wrote about what Kierkegaard said? "Life must be lived forwards, but it can only be understood looking backwards."

The interesting thing about freedom is that often the things that used to bind us and hold us down in our lives seemed like they kept us from being free. In hindsight, looking back at them, however, it may appear to be just the opposite. Sometimes, these challenges were just the things that we needed to grow and mature into new people. It may be financial hardship that leads to our spiritual evolution, for instance. Or a brush with death encourages you to pursue your dreams. If you look back on some of your challenges in life, you'll see a lot of them have led you to a better position today. Without those obstacles, you may have never weaved around to the road that you are currently on.

As Tony Robbins says, if you want to blame someone or something for your failure or your lack of progress, you also have to thank these people or circumstances for your success.

. . .

It was just before 10 o'clock on a Thursday night when I turned to kiss my wife goodnight. It was part of our weekly ritual. Now, before you jump to conclusions about what that ritual is, I should probably tell you that my son has hockey practice at 6 am every Friday, so we go to bed as early as we can on Thursdays. On those mornings, I'm up and ready by 5 am to hit the road. Friday is my day off but, instead of spending it sleeping in as most people would, I choose to invest that time into my son's future.

However, it wasn't always like this. I used to spend Friday mornings hungover from the night before, looking for someone to blame last night's drunken mistakes on. I used to wake up feeling sorry for myself and not even realizing it. I'd spend weekend after weekend looking to cheat on my wife (at the time) or wishing that I could find someone to cheat on her with—I wasn't a model husband.

It's still hard to believe that my life has changed so dramatically over the years. It's also hard to imagine that these weekly early-morning pilgrimages will one day be a distant memory. Someday, I hope my son will look back on them fondly as valuable time he got to spend with his old man.

Each week, my son and I reach uncharted territory in our conversations. We push ourselves to explore new ground in our morning dialogues and we both learn something about ourselves in the process. Unlike talking with clients, speaking with my son is a time for me to learn. I spend all of my week guiding and teaching and, while I learn a great deal from my clients daily, I am being paid to be the role of a mentor figure.

The innocence of children has a way of turning the tables on you and rearranging what you thought you knew about yourself. It is on these pre-dawn drives that I am reminded by my eleven-year-old son's inquisitiveness that I never had a father figure to teach me these lessons. Instead, I plunged forward without any paternal wisdom to guide me. As a result, I never learned how to treat people, how to truly care for a woman, or how to love and respect myself, for that matter. I only learned how to take the easy route. The rest I learned the hard way. I never thought I'd say it, much less write about it in a book, but staring at my son over in the passenger seat, I'm grateful for every mistake I have ever made. If for no other reason than that I can pass on the baton of fatherly wisdom and save him from making the same poor choices...

Today's drive is pretty silent. Static scenery shifts places. Trees bleed into green traffic lights and shimmering neon signs for businesses that won't be open for another four hours glow in the pre-dawn moonlight. I look at my son; he's engaged with a lighted-screen. As I keep my eyes on the road, I feel a strong connection to Will. He's getting what I never had: a father to coach him, to love him, and to see him grow up and become a strong young man. I look back over and offer him a reassuring smile. His face lights up, this time not from his cell phone screen, but from the trust and love that we've built in our relationship.

Our gentle glances quickly swerve into deeper territory as he asks me a question that makes me nearly run us off the road. I take a deep breath and try to center myself. His words cut me a second time.

"Hey Daddy, what made you have three divorces before Mama?"

"Oh, boy. That's a doozy, son. " I think to myself, trying to find the right words and discernment to put this into context for my nearly twelve-year-old son. Growing up in a world rife with social upheaval and change, I try to find something that will stick with him. I want him to have something that he can take with him—even remember for the next fifty years—the kind of pep talk you see in the movies that I wish my father would have given me.

I take another big breath and say a silent prayer that my lips will find the right words. Still wet with my morning energy drink, my mouth begins formulating words.

"Son, your father was a victim."

"Like someone robbed you?" Will's face wrinkles with worry.

"Not quite like that, Will. What I mean is that I felt like other people were always the bad guy. I felt like I was always getting hurt by the world. I had an attitude that made me feel like I was being wronged."

"Like a mindset?" he says, cocking his head sideways, still a little unsure of himself.

"Yeah, just like in hockey. My mindset was that I thought everyone else was wrong and that I was right."

"You mean you blamed them? Is that what happened with Grandma G?"

"That's right. I blamed Grandma G for many years." I catch a glance of my eyes in the rearview.

"But why did you have three divorces—did you blame those on Grandma G, too?"

"Partly. Will, when someone wants to be a victim, it doesn't matter what other people do or don't do. A victim will always find a reason to feel like it wasn't their fault. No matter what."

"But why would anybody want to be a victim? I don't understand." He presses his lips to his blue Gatorade.

"Well, you see, there are lots of reasons why people like your dad choose to be victims in life. Would you like me to tell you about them?"

He nods enthusiastically. Will likes to learn. That's one trait that he got from me.

"Okay, we have a while to drive, so let's get into it..."

I check my face in the rearview mirror once more. I've come a long way these past few years. I never thought I'd be sitting in this truck telling my son that my mother wasn't the problem. I never thought I'd be taking responsibility for my actions. Frankly, I never thought I was the problem or that I needed to change.

Some days, I still get goosebumps thinking about the ways that I have helped my counseling clients. I'm grateful that I am even in a place where I can offer that level of assistance and service. I glance back at Will; he's biting into an apple for some pre-practice B vitamins. I'm hoping that he takes after his mother and that, in this case, the proverbial apple falls far from his father's tree.

"Okay, so first things first, you are not going to get this right all of the time, son. Throughout your life, as soon as you think you have this figured out, as soon as you think you've got this, that's the exact moment that you will run into problems. Just like in hockey, the moment you take your eye off the puck, that is when things go sideways. Another way to say this is that you need to live intentionally. Do you know how to do that?"

"By doing what you want all the time?" He begins snacking on his lunch. He sinks his mouth (baby teeth and all) into his sandwich.

"Don't eat that yet."

He looks back at me, puzzled, his mouth half-full of turkey, before slowly sliding his sandwich back into the bag.

"Not quite. You see intentionality is like this—if you eat your sandwich now, your stomach will hurt when you get to practice, and then you won't have anything to eat later when you're really hungry after practice. Being intentional sometimes means you have to save that sandwich for later because you know you'll need to eat it then. Even though you want to just eat it right now. That's what most people don't understand. When you are really intentional, you are grateful for what you have and you are content with the progress you are making. If I'm not grateful and I am not content, then I can never be happy."

Will's eyes are wide awake now. He's tracking everything I'm saying. "Do you know about forgiveness, Will?"

He nods.

"Everyone does. But what most don't know is that forgiveness starts with you forgiving yourself for not being perfect and for not always having the right answers. It means forgiving yourself for screwing it up and making mistakes. When you live in this world of forgiveness, there's a world of acceptance that opens itself up to you. Those are the two concepts that make all of this other stuff work. Son, there are no enduring relationships without forgiveness."

My phone chirps at me. My eyes quickly glance at the message as my phone sits on the dash. "Will, where are your clean clothes for after practice?"

"I don't know."

"What do you mean you don't know?"

"Well, Mom didn't wash them for me like she usually does. So, I don't have anything to wear." "I know, Will. Mom just texted me and told me. So, whose fault is that, Will? Yours or Mama's?"

"Mama's," he says, without skipping a beat.

"Why?"

"Because she didn't wash them."

"Is that your job or Mama's?"

"Mama's."

"You see, Will, blame is when the problem is OUT THERE—somewhere outside of me—that's what victim mentality is. It's not my fault, it's Mom's fault."

"But..."

I raise a finger to silence him.

"Blame is when you say, 'If they would just do this, then I would be able to do what I need to do.' There's no power in that. With blame, the word that comes up a lot is responsibility. Responsibility is a good thing, Will. It means that you take ownership of what you do and how you impact people. In 2006 I got fired from US Cellular—it was all my fault, but I wasn't seeing that I was—"

"So why is it my fault that I don't have my school clothes? Mama washes my laundry."

"Yes, she does. But did you bring her your clothes last night and ask her to wash them?"

He shook his head.

"You see, Will, you had an expectation that Mom would just behave in a certain way. And when she didn't, you blamed her for her behavior instead of taking responsibility for your behavior. Expectation really runs the show for most people. If other people don't treat them kindly or don't do things the way they thought they would, a lot of people get fired up about that because their expectations aren't being met. As a result, they miss out on so much in life because it doesn't go just how they thought it would. My expectations are mine. People get so attached to normalcy."

He is turned away from me now, his cheeks and nose glued to the cold glass window.

"In our house, Mama doesn't wash the clothes because that's her job. Mama washes them because she chooses to. She can stay up later than I do on Thursday nights because I have to drive you to practice the next morning. So, if she needs to wait on your laundry, she can get it done and still get her rest. There is also an expectation on you, Will, that you get your laundry to your mother so she can do it for you. If you don't do that, then the expectation is that you will do your own laundry. You don't have to have your mother wash your clothes for you. You expect them to be done by her, but you are also choosing for her to do them."

He is still staring out the window.

"Do you see that, Will? Does that make sense to you?"

The whirr of the wheels on the road is all that echoes back to me. I can tell he is feeling guilty.

"Up until a few years after you were born, Will, I really struggled with guilt and shame."

"Why, Daddy?" his head swivels back toward me.

"I was incredibly hard on myself, son. My self-talk was crazy. I'd call myself a cheater, a liar, and I felt very shameful about my past. I wasn't faithful in any relationship I was ever in. It always made me feel bad to think about it. I'd think about how I should have known better or I'm such a bad person, with all of these feelings, guilt was always in control of me. When guilt is in the driver's seat, it keeps us upset and oppressed. Regret is a worthless emotion because it doesn't change anything. Guilt only makes you feel more guilty—it makes you feel ashamed. That's all it does. Ever. Nothing good ever comes from feeling guilt."

I lean over and squeeze his shoulder gently.

"I can be sorry or I can feel sorry for how someone was hurt by my actions in the past". Carl Jung says that, when you get to the point where you have total acceptance of who you are—the good parts, the bad parts, the light, and the dark—that's when you start getting healthy. That's where inner peace comes in. So it's okay if you feel sorry for something that you did, like we talked about the other day. It's not okay if you feel worthless because of it, though. Does that make sense?"

"I think so," he squeaks timidly.

"That's okay; it will make sense when you're older. And I will keep reminding you. Will, have you ever felt like you just have too much homework, too many hockey games, and haven't slept enough?"

He had just told my wife that he felt that way the night before.

"Well, a lot of people feel like that every single week, Will. We call that feeling being overwhelmed. Being overwhelmed is working 80 hours a week and feeling like you need to be everything to everyone."

"Were you overwhelmed, Dad?"

"I was, Will. Part of what helped me to take back control of my life was setting boundaries. Being overwhelmed comes from a lack of boundaries. As a sales manager, there was no vacation for me. You were too young to remember those days but, when I didn't answer the phone or I didn't have a solution for someone else, it made me feel like I wasn't enough. It made me feel like there is something more that I could or should be doing."

"Is that how Mama feels sometimes?"

"It's how we all feel sometimes. Remember the other day, when you didn't score that goal? The whole team was so excited that we won but you were still upset. You felt like you weren't enough. Will, you can't score the winning goal every single time. Michael Jordan took the final shot when the game was on the line and a lot of times, he made it, but there were also several times that he missed. Do you remember what I told you?"

He shakes his head "No."

"I told you to always do your best. That's all you can ever do, Will. But when you've done your best, you need to be happy with the results—whatever they are. Being overwhelmed is when you beat yourself up for unrealistic expectations".

"Everyone's expectations will be different, so you can only judge yourself based on your own set of standards. I remember that fourth grade was the first year I brought home a D on my report card."

Will looks at me in disbelief. His eyes grow wide.

"Grandma G was really mad at me. She said I don't care what you get as long as you get a C or higher. I bet that sounds pretty weird to you, Will, because your mom and I are always expecting so much more from you. But Grandma G didn't expect much of me. She didn't ever think I'd be where I'm at today. This is what I learned, Will. That experience taught me that all I needed to do was just enough to get by. That showed up everywhere for me in my life. I did just enough to be good. But I would never do the extra work to be great."

"Is that why you always make sure I do my chores the right way each week?"

"Yes, because how you do one thing in your life is how you do everything. Something as simple as replacing a paper towel roll. I wouldn't even put it in correctly. I was too lazy. That's why I am always making sure you do things the right way. I want you to feel good about what you are doing because you know you aren't cutting corners like your dad did."

Thinking about those times in my life is tough. I was so apathetic, so unwilling to put in any effort.

"Will, it's really easy to say that you are confused and not do your homework. Or, tell your coach you didn't understand something after you do it wrong. But, at some point, confusion is nothing more than just an excuse. What's something that you are confused about? Give me an example."

"Dad, what's the right way to be a good person?"

I swallow the rest of my energy drink in one big gulp. What a question!

"Well, that's a very interesting question, son. When we think in terms of 'right or wrong' we get stuck in judgment. I used to be a judging machine. Everywhere I went I thought I knew better than everyone else. I didn't understand that I was judging them. Today, I no longer make people right or wrong. I don't think that there is right or wrong, Will, aside from basic human morality. I just believe in seeing if it works for people. Does it get the job done? Then, that's okay with me. If we think that our way is the only way, then we can't be with other people who do things differently."

"Why do people make other people right or wrong though, Dad? I don't get it. Does what they did before make them bad today?"

"That's a great question, Will. Most people let the past dictate what is right or wrong for them. They believe that what happened in the past is exactly what will happen again. They have resentment. They have resignation. They are cynical—they are bitter and doubt whether anyone can ever change..."

"Why?" Will's eyes look very puzzled. He looks so innocent as he sits there, and I realize that he probably hasn't encountered the cynical side of life yet at his age.

"For some people, it is easier to believe that they can't change than it is to actually become a better person."

"But you changed. Didn't you Daddy?" His eyes are like little laser beams searching my soul for the answer.

"I did, son," I answer honestly.

"Then can't anybody change if they want to?"

"Yes, they can. But only if they really want to. All we can ever go by is what people do. Looking at my body of work before I was thirty, I was a mess. I was not to be trusted. I was not a guy that I would hang out with today or someone I would allow to drive you to hockey practice, Will.

"As you go through this life and you get rid of blame, you begin to get rid of guilt. When you get rid of guilt, you get rid of the power the past has over you, and that power that the past stole from you, begins to come back. Then you live in your power, Will, and you can keep being powerful no matter what anyone says to stop you.

"There are always choices that you can make to stay in control of yourself and not to let the past hinder you from living the life that you want. That's the power of being intentional. That's where free will comes in. Every person desires to let go of the pain of the past. Every person desires to let go of their painful childhood, failed relationships, and missed opportunities. However, what happens, Will, is that people get very attached to who other people used to be, so they keep them stuck there."

"Like Grandma G." Will is quick with that response.

"Yes, Will, just like Grandma G. It took her a long time to realize that I was a different person. It's very hard but, to let go of the past, you have to allow that other person to become someone else. Sometimes, they have to become an entirely new person in your eyes before that relationship can heal. This will make more sense to you when you are older, okay?"

Will nods and I can tell he's interested.

"People who are trapped in one of these seven victim mindsets don't know why they don't want to let go of these self-sabotaging perspectives. It feels very real to them and they don't even know why. I think a majority of people have a negative outlook on themselves, whether it's fake humility or arrogance. They are victims and they don't even realize that they are playing the victim role."

We pull into the parking lot for Will's practice. It's still early as he gets out of the truck. He grabs his gear and runs inside. I sit in the parking spot and begin reflecting on our conversation.

What is freedom, really? A lot of my clients think that freedom comes when everything in their life has changed. They make the age-old mistake by thinking that, when their circumstances change, they will be free. In the stories I've shared throughout this book, one thing is for sure: When you do the internal work to create change in your life, your circumstances may change as a result. However, someone who is truly free doesn't need their circumstances to be different to be free. They can accept their reality exactly as it is and make the most of it. This is true freedom. Allow me to recap how this can be possible for you in your life.

A lot of people think that, if they leave an old relationship or let go of past trauma, they will heal the pain of the past. Simply removing painful stimuli can be a great step in creating energetic boundaries. However, it's not a foolproof solution. It's a quick and easy fix that many people aren't brave enough to even attempt for themselves. If I make the case against myself, I get to be the bad guy and I get sympathy for it. People are really just looking for avenues for themselves to get attention.

Change and Transformation

A lot of my clients get caught up between describing change and transformation. They misuse them interchangeably. So I tell them to use this little trick to remember the difference because not knowing the difference can hinder their progress.

If you change your hair, the likelihood that it can change back is pretty high. Unless your hair stops growing back, it will return to its original form. Transformation is like getting laser hair removal. It's unlikely you will ever revert to your old ways.

Acceptance is a choice and choosing to accept your past is a choice. Acceptance is a major key to happiness. This is how it is; this is where I'm at. These are the cards that I was dealt. I have to play these cards, even if I don't like them. I don't have a choice. I still have to play my hand to the best of my ability.

What I ask my clients is, "Why should you have known better? Based on what? How did you know to do better?"

When you stop to think about it transformational change can be really painful.

Growing pains hurt. Hard work hurts. Birthing something new into the world hurts a lot. During labor, the pain is so immense that women scream. Women say, "Oh my God, that was excruciating, I would never want to do that again." But what do we see women doing? The outcome is so worth the pain that women have multiple babies. They are willing to sign up for that outcome again, so they go through the pain of labor to achieve it.

Working out sucks, but the outcome is awesome.

Eating right sucks, but the outcome is awesome.

Change sucks, but the outcome of transformation that comes from that change is awesome.

Freedom Is the Abolishment of Fear

Freedom is having brand-new feelings about familiar topics. You don't feel the same about old patterns, old feelings, and old memories anymore. Very few people can access this. Many people are making a re-creation of the past and calling it a life.

It is not just their story—it is their enslavement. They are bound to the past and bound to stay stuck in the feelings of the past, which keeps them from being free. This is a choose-your-own-adventure—a dichotomy between two stories. One is a cautionary tale, the other is a tragedy that turns into a romance—a love story of appreciation and gratitude.

Freedom is a process. It's a process of working through all seven of these illusions. As we break through those illusions, we find our freedom. I can say with confidence that I don't blame anybody else for how my life goes because, when something happens, I affirm to myself that it had to be that way. That's the reality and you can't deny reality.

When I stopped resisting the notion that life shouldn't be the way it is, that was it for me. That's when the eureka moment happened. The light bulb clicked on. My task isn't to change other people's behavior anymore. My only job is to learn how to accept it so that I can move on.

Change is optional, but growth is always required.

What people said about you, what people thought about you, it is old news and really NONE of your business. When you break free from the constraints of your past, that's when life starts getting good.

When that happens, you are in what jazz musicians in the 1920s referred to as "being in the pocket." This is when you are feeling the rhythms of life. But this is not a one-and-done. That's not how this book works because that's simply not how life works. It is a consistent and constant "battle" to keep yourself moving forward. Life is always searching for balance and homeostasis but is a constant fluctuation.

That's where the power of this final lesson comes in. It is only in the freedom of everything being in flux that you finally start feeling powerful. When you face an old circumstance, when this comes up—I am typically not at my best, but when you face it and use these new tools—boy, that's when you can really step into your power and use your freedom.

Freedom is being able to deal with stimuli that used to trigger you, upset you, or hurt you and look them in the eye, with no change in your emotions or mental state. Real freedom is always emotional freedom. The biggest piece of that freedom is being free from fear.

I look over my shoulder as Will approaches the truck. Practice is over. He looks victorious. As soon as he gets in, he explains how he is making progress on his stick-handling. However, when he gets in the truck, I can tell something is on his mind.

"What are you thinking about, Will?"

"Well, I've gotten better at skating with the puck but it takes me longer to set up to shoot. I have to think about it more with this new form. I'm not as fast as I used to be, but I'm more accurate."

This is a common complaint of some of my therapy clients. When they begin a new way of being, it takes some getting used to.

"You are birthing the new you, which means you have to go through that birthing pain of healing your old bad habits. We can think about a butterfly struggling to get out of its cocoon. If I say, "Oh, that looks painful, let me help you," and I reach down and cut him out of his chrysalis do you know what happens to the butterfly?

"He falls to the ground and his wings will never be strong enough to fly, so he dies. The struggle to get out of the cocoon is what makes him strong enough to live in the world. Just like in hockey, your muscles aren't used to doing it this way yet. So they take some time to learn it. And, by going slow, you build up the muscles necessary to move really fast in the future—you'll have the ability to fly with the puck, Will!"

His eyes are lit up now. I can tell that this is really sinking in for him.

"All over the world, people are running around clipping other people's wings, Will. They think they are helping people, but they are becoming codependent; they aren't making choices, they are making decisions. Don't believe what you see around you, Will. In life, you'll step back and you'll look at the people, the places, and the things in your life and at one time or another it will all seem like problems. In those moments, when things are tough, do not believe the circumstances in your life. You are in charge of how you respond and react to what's going on. It may be slow at first but, once you learn to listen to yourself and to avoid falling into any of the seven victim mindsets, you will never be a victim of your circumstances.

"Always remember this: If you want to become successful, become a master at living your life with intention. When you live intentionally, you can create the circumstances you want but remember that, whenever things aren't how you want them to be, forgive yourself and forgive the other people involved. You are defined by how you react to your circumstances, not by what has happened to you.

"If I had let my circumstances define me, I wouldn't even be alive today. All of the cards were stacked against me, and yet I overcame. I learned how to become a Master of Circumstance, and one day, Will, you will, too."